Grading

James A. Bellanca is the Director of the National Center for Grading and Learning Alternatives, and is the author of Values and the Search for Self.

Grading

nea
National Education Association
Washington, D.C.

by
James A. Bellanca

Stock No. 1603-3-00 (paper)
           1612-2-00 (cloth)

Note

The opinions expressed in this publication should not be construed as representing the policy or position of the National Education Association. Materials published as part of the NEA Professional Studies series are intended to be discussion documents for teachers who are concerned with specialized interests of the profession.

Library of Congress Cataloging in Publication Data

Bellanca, James A   1937-
   Grading.

   (NEA professional studies)
   1. Educational surveys.   I. Title.   II. Series:
National Education Association of the United States.
NEA professional studies.
LB2823.B44   371.2'721   77-23218
ISBN 0-8106-1612-2
ISBN 0-8106-1603-3 pbk.

CONTENTS

INTRODUCTION: GRADING AND GARDENING

Not long ago, I was conducting a day-long seminar on evaluation options at the University of Wisconsin, Stevens Point. When my host introduced me, he wondered aloud why someone with a hobby like gardening (we had swapped gardening yarns the previous evening) and who was averse to tests and measurements, would become interested in finding alternatives to grading.

As I reflect on my first teaching years in Park Forest, Illinois, I remember how faithfully I practiced the skills learned in Dr. Hauge's Educational Measurement 202. My slide rule was well used. I red-marked my students' compositions (although I must admit the first 25 always seemed to get more thorough attention), I calculated my normative test scores (no electronic calculators in those days), and I detailed each quiz score, adding precise points up to the fourth decimal (sometimes the fifth!). No accountant kept more precise records. Dr. Hauge would have been pleased to recall that I was his A student.

Over the years, I refined my system. Sometimes I wondered whether the "throw 'em down the staircase" rule wouldn't have been more accurate and burned less midnight oil, but I never succumbed to *that* temptation—at least until my daughter Carla started school. In fact, all my children shared the responsibility. Until they started to school and I was forced to wear my school-parent hat, I was content enough to play the grading game, to garden, and to believe that grades had not much to do with education. But when I began to perceive the negative effect that grades did have on children, on my children, I could no longer hide behind the red pencil and the black book.

I am glad to say that my children have never received a grade, and they probably won't until they begin high school. Happily, we can deal with real issues at home, and in our parent-teacher conferences. In this past year, we have focused on Jamie's small muscle difficulties (he's a first grader) and the math he loves (my son, a math nut?), on getting Mary Jo less involved with books and more with other children (Mary Jo is a fourth grader in love with horses and horse stories), and on helping Carla finish her weekly goal contracts without cramming on the last night. (Carla is a middle schooler who loves school, her piano, and her friends, but also has self-expectations that leave her with more to do than she can fit into a week.) In between conferences, we've read some "fuzzies from teacher," shared several phone conversations, helped with homework, dried tears, reviewed stacks of completed workbooks, drawings, and tests, checked over daily records, and talked much together.

These experiences, combined with my increasing dislike for the responsibility imposed to evaluate students by standards that I found inadequate and often contrary to my own values, made me gradually aware that grades were counterproductive to all that I loved about learning. I decided to act. I saw no valid arguments to defend my continuing use of grades. If I could not tolerate grading foisted on my own children, I would not impose grades on others.

From that first decision of mine many changes evolved. The specific steps are not important. What is important, I think, is the process that has carried me to the point where I can say with conviction, "Grades, as used in 97 percent of our schools, are *the key factor* in the perpetuation of a schooling process which has failed to accomplish its own expectations." I need not cite the unhappy facts of illiteracy, conflict, and teacher despair that characterize our schools. Parents, students, and teachers are trapped in a system in which the real, but hidden agenda is control, not learning, and where the ultimate weapon of control is the grade.

Those who support traditional grading will argue that the fault rests with the teachers (always convenient scapegoats), rather than with the grading system itself. This argument, wrongly, I think, idealizes the teacher as a being with no faults, no weaknesses, no personal opinions—a fantasy of perfection. But grading forces every teacher, no matter what her/his beliefs, to adopt an evaluation system the essence of which is to hamper, to devalue, and to destroy individual self-worth. No matter what good intentions a teacher caught in this system may harbor, or how she/he may play down the negative aspect of grades; no matter how the class may be involved in decisions about grading standards, or what humane strategies may be used to counteract the atmosphere, one bitter reality remains: at semester's end, the verdict comes, camouflaged as an A, B, C, D, or F.

Let there be no misunderstanding. I believe that grading is morally wrong, practically ineffective, and a major deterrent to learning. I believe that no teacher should be forced to grade, and no student be graded. These are basic rights. I do not say that evaluation is unimportant to the learning process. It is important. I do not suggest we sweep away grades with one immediate stroke. I do say that every teacher, student, and parent should strive to eradicate the grading game as quickly as practicable. With that key out of the lock, we can open the door to more successful teaching and more beneficial learning.

THE GRADED SOCIETY: AFTER ALL, EGG CRATES, MEAT SLABS, AND BUREAUCRATS ARE GRADED, AREN'T THEY?

At a National Conference on Grading Alternatives, a workshop leader asked audience members to describe or define grades in a school context.

> "It means to level. Grades level kids out."

> "Whenever my principal starts his bit about grades, we get hung up on efficiency. 'Let kids know where they stand,' he says. I picture my dad's egg farm. As kids, we had to snatch eggs out of the nest and take them to a sorting room. There, the giant, white eggs were stacked in AAA cartons. AA's and A's were shuffled into their special boxes. The speckled eggs were dropped into bins. They were shipped to the bakery. Solid browns were passed into the family larder. My principal is sold on the same system for grading. It's all very quick, clean, and efficient."

> "Ours is a bureaucratic society. Bureaucrats are divided by grades . . ."

> "Grades are my dad sitting in judgment at report card time. We were twelve. Each kid could expect either an allowance increase or isolation from attention and affection for the month."

> "The real world is a world of grades and classes. Grades and marks prepare students to live in a graded society. Everything in its place . . ."

> "I once remember taking my fifth graders on a trip to the packing house. Great slabs of raw meat hung from hooks. Three somber men in white coats poked, prodded, and marked each slab—a purple prime, choice, or whatever. That night I had to make out the semester grades. I didn't have a white coat."

> "If grades were good enough for me, why aren't they OK for my students? I survived grades . . ."

Ask about grades and you will receive a potpourri of responses. The confusion of associations with the word "grade" stems for the most part from a confusion of attitudes, experiences, values, and beliefs about what is important in teaching and learning. The result is a system that most clear-thinking teachers and parents know is a mess, but which few have the energy to combat.

> "I remember grades. I remember very well how grades pitted me and my four brothers against mom and dad. Each eight weeks was a battle of wits. We competed for rewards. Sometimes, knowing a bad report was on the way, I would race home to snitch the mail. I'd doctor the report and slip it back into the pile before dad read the mail. I wish my children wouldn't have to experience all that lying and cheating. But what else is there? Grades are like the plague. Nobody wants them, but who knows how to get rid of them?" (from a parent's letter).

Grades and marks, as any student in the last three generations will attest, are an established American tradition. After the surge to urban centers spelled the demise of the one-room school house in the early 1900's, the push for *efficient* institutions created administrative bureaucracies of increased complexity, including neatly printed grade cards. So rapidly did the graded report card take firm root that by 1911 the first major research project's negative conclusions could not destroy it.[1]

In the years from 1911 to 1960, school systems toyed with various letter and number reporting systems. Although research continued to show that grades were damaging to the educational process, only superficial changes were conceived. A classic example was in the Philadelphia experience. Between 1910 and 1960, the Philadelphia elementary schools floated from a 1 to 10 number system to denote all-around progress and letter grades for conduct (1913-22), a five-letter code by subjects (1922-34), a three-symbol approach (1934-40), a two-letter approach (1940-48), a four-letter approach (1948-54), and a five-letter approach (1954-60).

In the 1960's, the struggle to humanize schools burst into a two-pronged attack on grades and marks. In the colleges, the students' battle for power forced the "relevancy" issue on unheeding faculty. Pass/Fail course options, written evaluations, and competency evaluation systems were introduced on big and small campuses. For the most part, the supposed innovations reflected the superficial "fiddling" experienced by high schools and elementary schools in the first half of the century: the letters changed, nothing more. (Yale University played the game adroitly. Yale shifted from ABCDEF to P/F. Within a few years, P/F gave way to Honors, HP, P, and Fail, without a computed grade point average. In the early 1970's, ABCD returned. In 1975, the F returned!)

In the elementary and secondary schools, a second and more significant attack on grading took place. At the elementary level, a variety of reforms tangential to the grading issue gathered momentum under the humanistic flag. The open classroom and British infant schools stressed personalized instruction; confluent education called attention to the integration of subjects and disciplines into coherent instruction of the child as a whole rather than as a collection of isolated skills. The quest for a clarification of values pushed learning beyond the narrow scope of facts and figures to the application of abstract ideas in the solution of personal and practical life problems. Motivated by these and other approaches which "gave legitimacy" to feelings, attitudes, beliefs, and values in the classroom, school systems sought new ways to organize and to administer individualized instruction. Many elected to follow the behavioral path. Guided by Bloom and Mager, (with a special boost from state legislatures bent on efficient accountability), school systems as large as that of Chicago and as small as Anoka's, in Minnesota, devised "continuous progress" instruction. In continuous progress, each student can progress at her/his own learning rate through a step-by-step scale of learning objectives. Specific objectives spell out what the student must master at each step. To master means to demonstrate that he or she has learned the idea or skill delineated in a specific learning objective. For instance: in the following scale, no student could move from step 1 to step 2, until she/he could show the teacher that step 1 had been attained according to the criteria. *Ideally, if the student cannot move to step 2, it is the teacher's responsibility to find a different way to help the child succeed.*

STEP 1: The student will understand the concepts of zero and whole numbers.

Mastered | X |

STEP 2: The student will understand place value.

Mastered | X |

STEP 3: The student will add and subtract up to three place numbers.

Mastered | X |

Continuous progress assumed many forms: teacher-made objectives and materials, prepackaged reading and math curricula (for example, the Ginn basic composition and IPI mathematics) or all school conversion plans (for example, the IGE approach from the Wisconsin Research and Development Project).

At the secondary level, the thrust against grading was advanced most strongly by the public alternative school movement. Initially a reaction against the "dehumanization" associated with public schools, the alternative schools assumed a radical, free school stance. As the need for a separate identity subsided, alternative schools became more utilitarian and practical in character, basing their attitudes on humanistic learning principles. Rather than the absence of all structure prevalent in the free school, alternative schools developed structures and support systems which gave first priority to student needs. Several districts, most notably Berkeley, California, and Quincy, Illinois, devised multialternatives. Each optional school developed a coherent philosophy, methodology, and structure that matched the needs of its population. (At Quincy, students may elect a structured program with its traditional courses; an individualized program that uses contract learning and self-pacing; an arts program that combines large and small group instruction; and a career program balancing in-school learning with outside-the-walls options.)

On the cutting edge of change and free from ponderous bureaucratic decision-making practices, alternative schools have supplanted the more traditional university lab schools as the prime creators of quality innovations. Examples abound. In the schools-without-walls, teachers have developed practical career-based options: internships, apprenticeships, and on-site instruction by business, professional, and industrial volunteers. In the SWAS (schools-within-a-school), teachers have devised interdisciplinary studies, a balanced emphasis on affective and cognitive learning, peer instruction, cross-age tutoring, parent-student-faculty involvement in decision making, instructional techniques based on needs, and the use of community volunteers.

The refinement of these teaching-learning options, which broke down the box structure of traditional schooling, supported the increasingly perceived need for evaluation methods suitable to new learning styles. Teachers asked: "If I individualize instruction, why must my evaluation remain comparative?"

In the late sixties and early seventies, other breakthroughs added impetus to the movement for workable alternatives to grades.

1. *Schools Without Failure.*[2] William Glasser described how failure in early schooling clouded the child's total school experience. For those who would argue that failure was an important learning experience, Glasser countered that failure only taught students how to fail. He implied that if we used the number of failures as a criterion of success, schools would merit top grades.

   To counter the hang-up with failure, Glasser proposed the school without failure. In that school, Glasser not only eliminated the F grade, but also added teaching strategies which would help students experience success. He advocated the "talk circle" based on his Reality Therapy techniques, teacher-student planning-conferences, and the elimination of punishment, preaching, and passive listening.

2. *Pygmalion in the Classroom: Teacher Expectation and Pupils' Intellectual Development.*[3] Rosenthal and Jacobson showed how IQ tests framed teacher expectations of students' learning. When told that certain students had high IQ's (they did not), teachers judged these students with the highest ratings

in all areas of performance including creativity and initiative. These higher ratings were attributable solely on the teachers' expectations for each child's performance and had no correlation with measured ability.

Since *Pygmalion,* other experiments have corroborated Rosenthals and Jacobson's "self-fulfilling prophecy." Although no formal research relating grades to teacher expectations has been performed, two teachers in Ohio did substantiate the relationship to their school board's satisfaction.

Sixty junior-high students were selected by computer to participate in the Ohio study. After two years, 30 had B or A averages in English and 30 had C or D averages. The high average students were assigned to a "regular" track class for junior English. The teacher was informed that placement tests indicated these students were "low achievers even for regular track and she should do the best she could." The low average students were placed in a "college-prep" track junior English class. The teacher was told that her students were "cooperative, hard-working, creative, and nice."

Even though the results were not derived from a formal research project, they were more than interesting.

	A-B Group		*C-D Group*
	High achievers described as "low achievers"		Low achievers described as "cooperative, creative, etc."
Year-end	A-0		A-3
grades	B-2		B-14
	C-19		C-12
	D-5		D-1
	F-3		F-0

3. *The National Conference on Grading Alternatives.* Taking a cue from *Wad-Ja-Get?,*[4] the Ohio Education Association sponsored a national conference to focus on the grading issue. More than 800 educators assembled in Cleveland to hear Neil Postman, Sidney Simon, Art Combs, and Rod Napier lead discussions and workshops. The conference attendees, not wanting its impact to die, organized the National Center for Grading/Learning Alternatives.

4. *The College Guide for Experimenting High Schools.*[5] The first commission for NCGLA was a research project. Conference participants and workshop leaders had perceived "college admissions" as a major obstacle to evaluation reforms. Real or imagined, the perception held by parents, teachers, and school administrators that colleges would not admit students without a grade-transcript or class rank, needed investigation. NCGLA surveyed 2,600 four- and two-year college admissions officers and 97 percent responded. Less than 3 percent required grades or grade-point averages for admissions. Among the four-year schools, applicants seeking "fair and equal" review without grades were encouraged to submit "more information, not less." SAT/ACT test results, written teacher evaluations, criterion lists, achievement test results, and essays were recommended by 77 percent of the four-year schools in this category.

Since 1974, NCGLA has cosponsored more than a dozen state conferences on grading alternatives. In two states,

Minnesota and Oregon, assisted by strong leadership from the state professional associations, follow-up conferences, and workshops have supported the local development of evaluation and reporting alternatives to grades. In Minnesota, the State Department of Education has added its resources by providing consultant support and project guidance to local districts which have used parent, teacher, and student input to devise alternatives to grades.

In some respects, evaluation and reporting are coming full circle to the pregrade impetus of the late nineteenth century. As parents call for involvement and accountability, as alternative schools return to the personalized classroom of the one-room school house, and as administrators discover that efficient comparisons do not guarantee learning, cooperative efforts to humanize evaluation and reporting give hope that grading will indeed apply only to meat packing, egg crating, and institutional bureaucracies other than schools.

MYTHS ABOUT GRADES: IF MYTHS WERE STRIKES, GRADES WOULD BE OUT

Remember Romulus and Remus? Sisyphus? Icarus? Zeus and Apollo? These were the characters of myth who intrigued our youthful imaginations. In childish delight, we believed these stories of fabled adventures in far distant places. To the ancient myths of Greece and Rome, modern school lore adds its own mythology, including multiple myths about grades.

The First Myth
Grades are Objective Reports

To demonstrate the so-called objectivity of grades, gather 25 or 30 teachers or parents together. Show the triangle diagram to the group and ask each person to count silently the number of triangles perceived. After three minutes, stop the count and tell the group that you are going to tabulate the results. List the numbers 1 to 30 so that all can see (overhead or blackboard). Call out each number and tabulate raised hands for each number. When the results are seen, ask the audience to explain the discrepancies. You might expect responses like these:

"I didn't *see* the small triangle in the center."

"I made a triangle in the lower right corner."

"I wasn't sure if the lines were straight."

"I didn't see all the combinations."

"I thought you wanted only the major triangles."

"I saw everyone else working and I kept plugging away to make sure I had more. I didn't want to be stupid."

"That's a triangle?"

. . . . and so on.

Objectivity versus subjectivity is a nonissue, especially when perceptions are involved. Aided by a precise, geometric definition, counting triangles should result in strong arguments favoring objectivity. Unfortunately for those who would worship objectivity, individual perceptions framed by physical location (distance, angle, light), personal experience (good and bad teacher, positive and negative feelings, chance to practice), individual needs (closure, anxiety, competitive achievement) and other influences shift the scale toward subjectivity, even when an objective subject such as math is considered. The problem becomes more complicated when people and grades are meshed.

The Case of Sally Sharp

Sally Sharp is a superstar as students go. She knocked the top off the California Test of Basic Skills, ranked number 1 in her class, and captained the girl's field hockey team. In the first quarter Sally earned straight A's in all subjects.

In the second quarter, Sally performed as follows in Civics:

1. She gave an excellent oral report to the class on the workings of the "check and balance" system. She used charts and a sound-slide show which she prepared.

2. Sally received 99 percent, the highest grade, on her U.S. Constitution test.

3. As an independent, extra credit project, Sally interviewed her legislator and designed a comic book which showed the legislator introducing a bill before the Senate.

4. Sally worked with a committee to present a debate—"Resolved: The President Must Exercise Moral Leadership." Sally's affirmative won.

5. During the final week of the third quarter, Sally decided to run for student council president. She was excused from class twice weekly to plan her campaign. As a result, she was allowed to postpone her quarter test, "The Roles and Responsibilities of the President," until after the election.

6. Because she was running for office, Sally believed that she could not offend other students in class. When controversial issues arose, she never expressed her personal views and sided with the majority, even when she disagreed in principle.

7. Sally's final quarter report, "The Decision To Withdraw from Viet Nam," was poorly researched. Although not up to Sally's usual standards, the report was one of the best in the class.

8. Sally was defeated for office.

9. Sally failed the makeup exam which she took the day after the election.

To move the objectivity-subjectivity discussion from triangles to students and grades, ask the teachers and parents to grade Sally on an A to F scale, and explain the grade. Record the grades and the explanations for all to see. Just as the Elliott and Starch study (p. 9) illustrated that each teacher would grade a common essay or math test by subjective standards, you can anticipate that your parents and teachers will assign to Sally different grades for different reasons. There is no way that a generalized symbol, be it an A, a C, or a Pass can *fairly* represent a compromise among class goals, individual ability balanced against achievement, teacher expectations, and the accompanying multitude of values, feelings, and beliefs which comprise a classroom. Without the compromise, the myth of grading objectively cannot represent reality. The objective grade is a myth.

The Second Myth
Students and Parents Want Grades

Picture 300 junior high school students gathered with parents in the local high school auditorium. On stage, two high school counselors prepare to answer questions and discuss "Preparing for High School." The hands wave.

(Q) "Do my eighth grade grades make any difference in what courses I take?"

(R) "Of course. Those with high grades in the last semester will have first selection for the high tracts. We will use your test scores and grades. These tell us who the interested students are."

(Q) "Does my level in high school have any effect on college admission?"

(R) "Most definitely. Your class rank is weighted so that an honors level A is worth more than a regular level A. You need to get your best grades now to insure higher level placement."

(Q) "Isn't an A in the second track better than an B or C in the honors track?"

(R) "I don't doubt that a college admissions officer takes most notice of how many A's there are. A's are always the best."

(Q) "If that is so, how can I be sure I will get in the level where I'll get the most A's?" . . . .

As the questions and responses pass, the tally of topics illustrates how students and parents demand grades, especially when the college admissions myth is reinforced by the school and community:

1. Grades (26 questions)

2. Tests (6 questions)

3. Discipline (2 questions)

4. Course options (1 question)

5. Alternative learning programs (3 questions)

6. Support services (1 question)

7. Other (3 questions)

Ironically, the evening session ended with contradictory counselor comments. On the one hand, parents were advised, "Don't respond to your child's wants." On the other hand, grades and tests were reinforced as "the evaluation system which parents and students want."

Aside from the contradiction, defense of grades based on "want" is a shallow argument. In one poll, students were asked to choose between grades and no grades. Obviously, the heavy majority opted for grades. What adult would select no salary if given the either-or choice—to work with pay or without pay? The students understand their reward system; grades are the open sesame to parental favor, allowances, peer status, weekend privileges, and dreams of college. Why surrender a possible kingdom for nothing?

What happens when students are asked to elect alternative *evaluation* methods not linked to a normative punishment-reward system? Research has given no clear answer to this question. One hint, however, comes from the experience of students in alternative learning programs. At John Adams High School in Portland, every student may elect grades in addition to written teacher evaluations. Less than 30 percent do so. At the Center for Self-Directed Learning in Winnetka, Illinois, students have decided by consensus not only to reject grades, but also to insist that all evaluators be trained to write evaluations and to conduct family conferences according to defined and acceptable criteria. These instances, like experience in other schools which give evaluation *options*, imply that students may "want grades" because grades are the only feedback tool they know.

The Third Myth
Colleges Require Grades

> "But colleges require grades."
>
> "But high schools require grades."
>
> "But junior highs require grades."
>
> "But elementary schools require grades."

The scapegoat string qualifies for what a five-year-old boy called "infinity plus one."

The college admissions myth is the base of the scholastic stepladder. At best, the stepladder demonstrates the possibilities for irresponsible scapegoating, "the (any name you want) school requires grades" rationalization. At worst, the stepladder serves to brainwash students into playing the "I Dream of Success" game; its whimsical rules, reinforced by bureaucratic administrators, support elitism and racism. Fears of failure manipulate parents and students away from learning and toward the superficial "wad-ja-get?" The kindergarten mania for letter grades "to prepare the child for elementary school" culminates in the business recruiter, who "must have grades."

If each passing on of responsibility to the next scholastic level were defensible in fact (what happened to that passion for objectivity?), the stepladder would stand. But the facts do not support any rationale given for the stepladder arrangement. The following arguments, supported by research and common sense, militate against the stepladder mentality:

1. Rosenthal and Jacobson's *Pygmalion in the Classroom*[3] counters these arguments in favor of grades. Strong support against grading young children comes from Glasser, Combes, Bloom and most other contemporary psychologists.

2. In December 1975, a study of criteria used by major corporations to recruit college graduates showed that grades were not the most important standard. Because the recruiters recognized the inherent unreliability of grades, they were more interested in appraisals, detailed and criterion based, of the candidates' personal qualities. About grades, one recruiter for a Fortune 500 company said: "Grades are a distant second. Grades say little. They are vague and unreliable."

3. Research studies have documented the unreliability of grades to predict success. The highest positive correlation shows that high grades indicate, as one might expect, that a student will earn more such grades at the next higher academic level. (They also show by inference, but never by direct statement, that low grades and failures continue at each

succeeding level of academia: D's and F's are permanent brands.) When the time comes for academic whizzes to enter the job world, grades not only fail to predict success, but they also demonstrate that "there was no relation between success as measured by grades in a school setting, and success in job performance ratings." In short, grades fail to prepare students for the world that exists outside the school walls.

4. Counselors for students of alternative high schools report that graduates have a college acceptance rate equal to or better than graduates in district traditional schools. Newton's Murry Road Annex, Chicago's Metro High, and Hartford's Shanti School have challenged the admissions myth and shown that a "no grades" transcript does not mean "no college admission."

The Fourth Myth
Grades Insure Competency

"Grades," writes a defender, "insure minimum competencies and basic skills." If grades do so, why do so many high school graduates lack the ability to write simple sentences or read at a sixth grade level? If grades insure competencies, why are employers harping on many employees' lack of basic math and reading skills? If grades communicate "mastery of the basics," why are parents crying "Back to the basics"?

Traditional grading, in many respects, must share responsibility for the death of competencies, especially in basic skills. A's, B's, and C's camouflage a multitude of sins. Because the letter grade is charged to accomplish everything from positive reinforcement to creativity to mastery of this course's skills, each teacher tries vainly to make the best decision for each child. For some teachers, the grade is the carrot; for others, the stick. In no two situations does the same grade mean the same thing. Unspecific, uninformative, subjectively judgmental, the grade cannot communicate accurately what skills each student has mastered. The results lead inevitably to high school graduates who cannot read street signs, complete tax forms, or pass a driver's test. Grades add up to incompetency.

If grades do not insure basic skill mastery or competency, what do they accomplish?

1. *Grades maintain a racist, elitist, and sexist educational system.* The All-American grading game has clear rules, all loaded to favor victory by the white, upper middle-class male. Although the American school system has assumed the appearance of democratic education, in reality it adheres rigidly to the nineteenth century principles of classical, aristocratic education. Just as blood and title predicted success at Oxford, grades and standardized achievement tests predict success at Harvard Law School.

Graduate school deans, relying on research which demonstrates that grades are the best predictors of academic success, start a chain reaction. Down the line, grades become a key weapon which allows teachers to shape and select who will advance up the ladder of success. Among the subjective reactions to grades are a host of culturally induced attitudes about sex, race, and class. From kindergarten upward, the selection process weeds out the female, the poor, the Black or Latino who doesn't fit subjective expectations. With the "objective grade" as defense rationale, dropouts and pushouts are scorned as "losers," girls are steered kindly into home economics and nursing, and the nonworshipper of books is directed—at age fourteen—into work training. (Even the House of Commons allowed its members to select their seats!)

The most virulent voices in defense of separatist grading practices are those parents whose children hold winning tickets. Grades equal passage up the corporate ladder. The success formula, a scholarly personification of the American dream, is simple: grades = $; $ = power; power = success. Not unlike the early Puritans who measured salvation by quantity of material goods owned, the grade-grubbing parent measures success by multiple A's on a report card. From kindergarten on, A's reinforce that Johnny is a good boy, playing the game, moving up the ladder to a select graduate school, a posh home in a protected suburban enclave, and a partnership in the prestigious law firm.

The story below, a version of a news item in a big city paper, illustrates all too vividly, the effect of grading on some students.

The "F" Tragedy

On his return from class at the local junior high on a Monday afternoon a few years ago, Jim Jones was holding a report card. It showed three F's, one C, and one D. He dreaded giving it to his parents.

At dinner that evening, when he broke the news, he was scolded, as his brothers and sister listened.

Shortly afterwards, Jim left the house alone. He did not come back.

Early next morning, a woman walking her dog in the park found Jim's body, hanging by a scarf from an iron railing.

Verdict: presumed suicide.

Presumed motive: despondency over school grades.

2. *Grades foster destructive competition.* The American character is forged in healthy competition. But when the sides are unevenly balanced, when some players have no chance to win, or when competition becomes the end-all, the American character is warped. What responsible coach would send an injured, unprepared, undersized, or out-of-shape player into the middle of the Super Bowl? What responsible business executive would gamble the company's future on an inexperienced or untrained salesperson? Yet, each day students without sufficient emotional or intellectual preparation are forced into competitive classrooms and told to "sink or swim." The results are as predictable as in business or sports. If the unprepared football player is not injured, he is discouraged; if the ill-equipped student is not overwhelmed, he or she lapses into apathy. Defeat begets defeat; failure begets failure. The last line of defense is passive anger, dropping out, drugs, and vandalism.

Because grades stress competition against external opponents, little school attention is given to internal competition. In the traditional school, discipline, responsibility, and goals are outer-directed; self-discipline, personal goals, and self-evaluation are ignored. In order to satisfy the voracious appetite of the great god Competition, successes and failures are the ultimate musts: for every winner, we *must* have a loser. After all, winning and losing—not self-disciplined learning— IS the name of the game.

3. *Grades create a Watergate morality.* Remember the surprise generated when the press revealed how "bright" Mitchell and Erlichman were? How could bright men commit flagrant crime?

Probably the least surprised group were law and medical students. They knew Nixon and his Watergate cohorts were men who had learned early in professional school that "dirty tricks" guaranteed a high rank in class. The name of the professional school game is "survival." "Get the other guy before he gets you." "Break lab equipment, steal notes, buy term papers." "Grades," commented a recent Harvard law graduate, "are the only things that count. Ironically, the people most likely to lead our state and federal governments, care for our sick, and operate our big businesses learn one key lesson: the end justifies the means. Does anyone with an ounce of sense wonder why cheating and conniving popped out in Watergate? I'm only surprised that they were dumb enough to get caught."

The following is a version of a news item that appeared nationally in the newspapers:

> The recent scandal at West Point involving cheating on the part of 90 cadets was a shattering event in the academy's long history. Is there a more telling comment on the pernicious influence of the struggle for good grades?

4. *Grades divide students and teachers.* The greater the grade pressure on students, the greater the division between teachers and students—the us and them syndrome. Grading is a depersonalized war game. Teachers use strategems to "keep kids in their place." Students design countermoves—selling term papers, cribbing, plagiarizing and making test files. Camps divide with teachers accusing each other of "lowering standards" and "kowtowing" and with students debating over "brownnosing" and "apple-polishing."

5. *Grades reduce learning to a survival of the fittest charade.* Learning, the quest to know and grow, is squeezed out of the classroom by the competitive battle for grades. When students are compared one to the other, winning and losing becomes more important than ideas and skills. Fawning, cheating, and stealing to get top grades take priority over working together, mastering skills, and exploring new ideas. For those who achieve top marks, the lesson is clear: survival means copping a grade. To those who garner D's and F's, learning means "honesty doesn't pay"; for those with average grades, the lesson is "sit still and accept the fact that you will always be a C student who sees life in average ways." Few learn to risk new insights, inquiry, discovery, honesty, or creativity. To the grade grubber, not to the learner, go the spoils.

6. *Grades devalue self-worth.* One of the more gruesome Greek myths depicts Orestes hounded day and night by the Furies. When Orestes sought sleep, the Furies attacked; when he hid, they pursued him into the darkest caves. For Orestes, there was no rest, no comfort, no sleep.

Every learner has furies, the personal put-downs that pursue relentlessly from the incidents when teachers and peers dictated, "You stink in math." "Who said you could write?" "You're stupid." "You're ugly." Through life each of us fights to escape our furies, but they tirelessly pursue. Like Orestes, we cannot escape them, the put-downs we learned through criticism provided by well-meaning teachers and friends.

Although most teachers learn that a positive self-image is essential to school success, the fury syndrome *sneaks in* at a young age. Red pencils slash, check, cross out. "No," "Wrong," "Minus 5" dominate the vocabulary, as if there must be graphic justification for the letter grades which dominate classrooms.

Grades teach students to deny their self-worth. On the one hand, high grades brainwash students to latch onto the teacher's judgment. "Teacher is right. Teacher is more educated. Teacher knows best." Students in this group, especially those with high dependency needs, become pawns. Only the A matters. A equals attention. Independent judgment, inquiry, and creative problem-solving are spurned for the direct support from the grade crutch. With all worth derived from the grade, the student says "I alone am nothing. I am the badge I wear, the grade I get."

At another extreme, grades produce the outcasts. Failure, as research indicates, produces more failure. The F syndrome never changes course. In the early years, the F indicates "You are wrong. To be wrong is bad. You are bad." In junior high, the pressure for inclusion mounts. The F outsiders, already labeled "bad," work to justify their common bond. Delinquent behavior, vandalism, drug and alcohol abuse are the rationalizations which call attention away from the academic nonachievement.

In high school, solidly formed into a social group with strong antischool feelings, the nonachievers reinforce the low academic expectations predicted for them by junior high counselors. Having gained the image, these nonstudents work diligently to maintain their open hostility and poor grades.

In between the superachievers and the antiachievers are the average students. Branded with the scarlet C, these students are expected to be dull, uncreative, and uninterested. Rather than openly rebel, the C folk sit mired in an apathy. Neither learning nor grades have meaning for C folk.

In no case do grades indicate that a student is an individual person with unique capabilities. Instead of recognizing that a finely tuned musical ear could develop into supreme musical talent, or a sharp eye for perspective could lead to a master carpenter, grades tell students how they don't belong or fit into preset molds. In essence, grades demonstrate that a feeling of individual self-worth counts less than conforming to group norms defined by the school.

Is it surprising, then, that some school districts report an alarming rise in the number of dropouts? In one Middle Western suburban county, a survey of the public high schools revealed that in the 1974-75 school year, nearly 6,000 students had dropped out. A breakdown of the figures showed the following motivations:

Lack of interest — ca. 3,500 students

Salaried employment — nearly 800

Poor health — ca. 150

Marriage or pregnancy — over 200

Military service — over 200

Expelled — nearly 140

Other (usually, no reason) — about 1,000

This county's superintendent of schools speculated that even more than 3,500 students had left from lack of interest. The survey demonstrated, he declared, the pressing need for alternative forms of education.

7. *Grades keep teachers in line.* To perceive how insidiously grades wreak havoc, a teacher need only recall the first months of teaching. With a freshly printed diploma, she/he entered the classroom blooming with new ideas, creativity, and dreams, dreams, dreams . . . but what happened? More than likely,

the first balloon prick came from the department head or principal. "Mr. Smith, you gave too many A's last quarter. May I see your grade book?"

Although most schools no longer measure accountability by the class grading curve (Too high? "You can't be a good teacher by giving easy grades." "There are departmental standards." Too low? "Watch out for parents calling the principal."), many principals and department heads collect semester grades and tabulate school and department curves. In one light-house high-school, the department head posts the department results with high, median, and low curves identified by teacher names. In each teacher's folder, she maintains a detailed record of the teacher's grade curves to use as "facts" in tenure and merit reports. She cannot understand why her department is rife with distrust and anxiety.

Grades coerce the recalcitrant and manipulate the dependent teachers. The real message communicated by grades is "Play the game by my rules, and I'll let you move ahead. Cross me, and I'll cross you out." In this way, grades do not insure teaching for mastery of basic skills, but do guarantee that the game players will rise to the top, the unsure will melt into middle-group apathy, and the creative teachers will drop out.

8. *Grades inflate themselves.* Like the economy, grades are beleaguered by inflation. In spite of scholarly pronouncements decrying the upward flow, nobody seems to know how to keep those grades in line. The Viet Nam War, bleeding heart professors, and various other excuses are sought for this, the second biggest problem to hit academia this year (the first is those test scores which are plummeting). In the desire to keep students (and as one university dean's memo gently implies, the faculty) in line, few are willing to consider the possibility that grade inflation is the direct result of the grading game. Having refined the weeding-out techniques which insure that only the best grade grubbers make it to college, the colleges are discovering that students are in fact not normatively curved anymore; well indoctrinated to the nuance of the game, these students have made the collegiate version of curved competition obsolete. The following is based on an actual newspaper article and illustrates this situation:

College Grades: Inflation Era

Some were born too early. For example, college students of the 1960's who fell into the C grade category. In 1976, those students would probably be rated B, or even A. It's a countrywide phenomenon. At Harvard, 82 percent of the class of 1974 graduated cum laude. At other famous universities, no one received an F, or in some places, not even a D. In fact, in one institution, 38 percent of the grades were A's.

All of this does not mean, unfortunately, that today's students are superior to their predecessors. It means that grades are in a state of inflation and that it is now recognized as a problem for educators. Grades are no longer reliable as an indicator of ability since graders are unwilling to assume responsibility for handing out poor or failing marks.

In baseball, everyone knows three strikes are out. The continued existence of grades, in spite of the research that has demonstrated their unreliability and nonvalidity, reveals the power and control held by an unfair reporting system which gives top priority to efficient record keeping. Efficiency is the life blood of any institution more concerned about its self-perpetuation than about the individuals it should serve. If there is enough efficiency, there will be little resistance from the victims—children, teachers, and taxpayers. Grades get A+ for efficiency.

EVALUATION CRITERIA: IF YOU GRADE THE
GRADERS, GUESS WHO FLUNKS?

Susan was angry. Her hand shook as she gave the green evaluation report to Mrs. Roland, her English teacher. Fighting back tears, Susan blurted: "I don't understand this report. You might just as well give me a grade. I worked hours to prepare a good self-evaluation and this is all the feedback I get."

A study of Mrs. Roland's written evaluation reinforces Susan's judgment; it provides no help for Susan in balancing her own perceptions with the insights and instruction of her teacher. If Susan were to evaluate Mrs. Roland's feedback according to the criteria for effective evaluation, Mrs. Roland would understand Susan's frustration.

Name: Sue Lauer   **Type:** Group-Directed Study

Evaluator: Mrs. Roland   **Title:** Poverty in America

Evaluator: Describe the students' learning according to the criteria established in the contract.

Susan was a positive member of the group. She did excellent work. She is a nice person, and I enjoyed working with her.

Mrs. Roland deserved Susan's angry blast and an F. The evaluation, as Susan had indicated, was less valuable than a letter grade. Like letter grades, Mrs. Roland's feedback was vague, judgmental, noninstructive, and not attuned to Susan's needs for specific feedback.

What constitutes an effective evaluation? What are the criteria that can help an evaluator provide helpful feedback? Is it possible to evaluate how we evaluate?

The Basic Criteria for Effective Evaluation

1.   *An effective evaluation is a sharing of specific information.* By sharing information, rather than by giving advice, an evaluator leaves the student free to select alternate improvement methods in accordance with personal needs and goals. When advice predominates, the learner is often placed in a totally "accept" or totally "reject" position. This, in turn, undermines the learner's trust in her/his capability to make personal decisions, arouses defensiveness, and stops self-evaluation.

Informative feedback has several advantages. If it is *descriptive* and *specific,* the feedback will give the student a concrete, detailed picture of what she/he has learned. Like a road map, descriptive specifics will detail exactly what learning she/he has completed. By measuring the completed learning against personal goals, the student will see for herself/himself what additional study is needed. Descriptive specifics, such as "mastered the use of coordinating conjunctions," reduces the student's need to respond defensively.

If the information provided is *well timed* and *in an amount that the student can use,* the feedback will not induce "overload frustration." In general, feedback is most useful when it follows immediately after the learning experience, not two months later. The timing is complicated by the learner's receptivity. To overload a person with feedback reduces her/his ability to use it effectively. An evaluator must exercise care that the timing and the intensity of feedback do not satisfy the evaluator's need to judge more than the student's need for assistance.

Meet Criteria	Do Not Meet Criteria
"In problem 2, the 9 and 7 are reversed. Here are some other ways to try the problem . . . ."	"Problem 2 is wrong." X
"I find that your sentence structure is more varied than in your last essay. For example, note the sentences I underlined in paragraph 3. You mixed the simple sentences with the complex sentences in accord with the patterns we discussed in class yesterday."	"Your sentences are better." B+ P

2. *A helpful evaluation is nonjudgmental.* In a nonjudgmental evaluation, the evaluator tries to accentuate perceptions without implying or stating absolute right or wrong. This avoids the horse-blinder point of view which forces the person being evaluated to become defensive toward negative judgments or overly dependent on positive judgments.

Meet Criteria	Do Not Meet Criteria
"This is how I perceive your difficulty . . . ."	"Your problem is . . . ."
"This is what I see . . . ."	"That was a bonehead approach."
"In this paper, I feel that you neglected the following rules of logic . . . ."	"Excellent" A

3. *A helpful evaluation clarifies in a positive and supportive tone.* Put-downs, ridicule, sarcasm, and negative distrust fail to recognize the student's worth as a thinking, feeling individual. Like an amoeba prodded with a pin, persons stung by a sardonic tone draw back. Defenses, which children erect against put-downs, inhibit the risk-taking so important in later learning.

Meet Criteria	Do Not Meet Criteria
"I appreciate your picking up all the blocks . . . ."	"That was a stupid thing to do."
"I am pleased with the higher scores you are making on the addition charts."	F
"I am unhappy with the lack of quotation marks on your papers. Can we talk about the problem I see?"	"Anyone with an ounce of sense would have studied for this quiz." "Why can't you wash your face like everyone else does?"

4. *A helpful evaluation provides options for remediation.* Evaluation is a power tool. It can manipulate students to act and to think only in absolutist terms as defined and controlled by the evaluator. This is the syndrome in which

every problem has one and only one correct solution. If the student strays from the true path, there are no options for remediation. Faced with dead ends, the student retires into apathy.

Meet Criteria	Do Not Meet Criteria
"Let's look at other ways we might work this painting."	"That flower should have had more red tint."
"Here are some optional methods you might use for writing your next paper . . . ."	B
"What other approaches can you list as alternative solutions to . . . ."	"Excellent work."

5.   *A helpful evaluation is based on standards of performance selected by the student and the evaluator in response to the expressed needs of each.* Clear and mutually selected criteria not only spell out specific expectations, they also build a feeling of cooperative trust and mutual respect between teacher and student. Unlike grades, which divide teachers and students into warring camps, promote cheating, and accent "wad-ja-get?," evaluations based on coselection of criteria build a classroom atmosphere that encourages students to focus on learning, care about each other, and seek creative solutions to problems. The norm is cooperation, not superficial and destructive comparison.

Meet Criteria	Do Not Meet Criteria
"The criteria for helpful evaluations—	"Very good work"
1. Are specific/instructive	
2. Are nonjudgmental	D
3. Are mutual criteria	
4. Are positive	"Compared to everyone else, your work
5. Provide options."	was excellent."

In traditional use, all evaluation is a judgmental process. Evaluation, using comparative norms, separates good from bad, winners from losers, successes from failures, and reports the results succinctly and efficiently. But, as the criteria for effective feedback imply, judgmental evaluations based on comparative norms do more to undermine the learning process than to help it.

Because today's learning is no longer limited to memorization and simple skill completion tasks, the traditional evaluation is an outdated tool. By continuing to rely on grades, grade point averages, and class rank, high schools and colleges not only perpetuate an aberrant mythology, they reinforce the problems about which teachers complain most: apathy, unskilled workers, grade inflation, and students unprepared in basic skills. Clearly, schools which rely on normative evaluations may be compared to GE or GM using treadmills to power their factories.

Nonjudgmental, criterion-referenced evaluations not only provide specific standards for performance, but also helpful feedback. In the criterion approach, each student can learn to set goals according to personal need and progress at a rate that he or she can handle. Additionally, if institutions must set admissions standards, the individual has the charge to prepare to meet those standards. If specific criteria such as the ability to write precise sentences, compose a unified paragraph, identify and use geometric laws, or read at a given comprehension level were detailed by each college, high school, or business, applicants would have clear guidelines. As it stands now, admissions officers and employment counselors depend on unreliable grades and test scores that communicate only the broadest, most universal, and nonpractical expectations.

To meet the criteria for effective feedback, schools and colleges must undergo several fundamental attitude changes:

1. In the early formative years (K-8), give only criterion-based, non-judgmental feedback and use individualized reporting methods that reinforce each child's positive self-image as a thinking, feeling, and deciding person.

2. Each high school must decide its own criteria for student placement in courses. By developing criterion-referenced tests and family entrance conferences, decisions for placement in specific programs (remedial, vocational, special education), ability levels, or courses will more accurately meet student and school needs than reliance on letter grades.

3. Clear, precise, and specific criteria for a high school diploma based on demonstrated knowledge and mastery of skills must be established. The minimum standards for the diploma could well reflect the California plan: the student must read, and complete all forms requisite for social survival: driver's license, income tax, social security, etc. Students who can complete the bureaucratic paperwork merit the diploma, and may leave school; those who choose to stay may work for a certificate of higher competencies, prepare for college, or train for skilled jobs.

4. Each college and university should develop its entrance competencies, not on having taken courses Y and Z, not on a vague floating GPA (the cutoff varies each year), but on a student's demonstrated ability to read, write, and analyze, at a specified, tested level determined by each college's faculty. In essence, each admissions office would need clear, published criteria for expected admission competencies and a method to test those competencies.

These four changes could alter American education from a pass-through, amass-up system of credit bargaining to a system relying on clear expectations and exact standards. The clearer the expectations and the more exact the standards, the more successfully students could set accomplishable goals and make personal decisions about learning. At the very least, these changes would ensure an evaluation-reporting system which does all that it claims to do. In a more optimistic view, the changes will cause the demise of passive, apathetic attitudes and make learning a meaningful growth experience for all students.

APPROACHING EVALUATION: WITHOUT GRADES, WHAT'S LEFT?

EVALUATION

There are three primary approaches to evaluation: the comparative or normative method, the criterion-referenced method, and the self-evaluative method. Although each shares characteristics of the others, each is essentially unique.

Evaluation: Normative Method

1. Compares students within a class, grade level, or school. Comparisons are determined by preestablished standards of group performance. A grade indicates a degree of achievement by each individual in relation to all others in the group or class. In the most stringent use, comparisons are curved in a bell. At each juncture on the curve, a predetermined number of grades is allowed (for example, 2 A's, 4 B's, 12 C's, 4 D's, 2 F's).

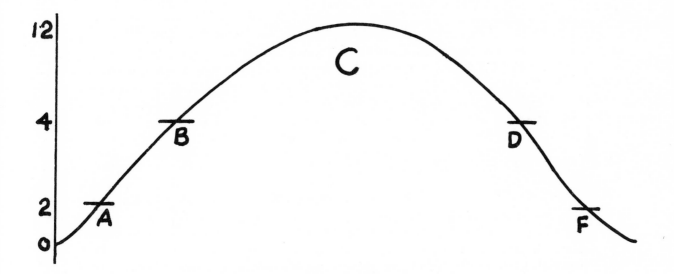

2. Motivates externally on the assumption that each learner has equal capability, the carrot A and the stick F are supposed to motivate each student to "do better."

3. Provides quantifiable information as a basis for a *summative* judgment. Focus is on the production of a tangible product which the teacher can measure and evaluate. If a product is not measurable, it cannot be graded.

4. Evaluates and reports as a single process separate from the learning process. The grading procedure does not meet feedback criteria.

5. Provides generalized education programs based on so-called expert assumptions about learner needs.

Evaluation: Criterion-Referenced Method

1. Establishes specific criteria for mastery of individualized skills and concepts. Allows for a spectrum of standards relative to performance quality. Individuals measure own achievements against unchanging standards, rather than by comparison with others' achievements.

2. Stresses internal, goal-set learning based on individual needs and abilities.

3. Provides quantifiable and qualifiable information for feedback. Can focus feedback on processes or products as long as criteria are clearly identified in learner behaviors.

4. Evaluates and reports as distinct processes. Evaluation based on effectiveness criteria for helpful feedback. Reporting methods vary and may meet effectiveness criteria.

5. Provides individualized learning options based on expert assumptions about learner needs.

ARITHMETIC SKILLS (3-4-5-6)

	I	II	III	IV
GENERAL UNDERSTANDING				
Knows 100 basic + facts in 4 minutes (5th).				
Knows 100 basic -- facts in 4 minutes (5th)				
Knows 100 basic X facts in 4 minutes (5th)				
Knows 100 basic facts in 4 minutes (5th)				
Can read and write 1 to 6 place numbers (4th) . . 2				
Understands place value (4th) 4				
ADDITION				
Adds correctly without carrying (3rd) 6				
Adds correctly with carrying (3rd). 8				
Adds 3 to 5 place numbers (4th) 10				
Adds ragged columns (5th) 12				
Writes and adds money (5th) 14				
SUBTRACTION				
Subtracts correctly without borrowing (3rd) . . .16				
Subtracts correctly with borrowing (3rd). 18				
Subt. 4 place nos. with zero in subtrahend(3rd).20				
Subt. 4 place nos. with zero in minuend (4th) . .22				
Subtracts money (5th) 24				

ARITHMETIC SKILLS (3-4-5-6)

MULTIPLICATION & DIVISION
Can estimate products (3rd) 26
Multiplies with 1 place multiplier (3rd). 28
Can estimate quotients (3rd). 30
Divides with 1 place divisor (4th). 32
Multiples with 2 place multiplier (4th) 34
Divides with 2 place divisor (5th). 36
Divides with 2 place quotient (5th) 38
Divides with 3 place quotient (6th) 40
Multiplies with 3 place multiplier (6th). 42
Multiplies with zero in multiplier (6th). 44
Multiplies with zero in multiplicand(6th) 46
Multiplies money (6th). 48
Divides with zero in quotient (6th) 50
Divides with 3 place divisor (6th). 52
Divides money (6th) 54

FRACTIONS
Knows fraction terminology (5th). 56
Draws simple fractions (5th). 58
Finds fractional parts of whole (5th) 60
Reduces fractions to lower terms (5th). 62
Changes whole numbers to fractions (6th). 64
Changes improper fractions to mixec numbers(6th).66
Changes mixed numbers to improper fractions(6th).68
Finds common denominator (6th). 70
Adds fractions (6th). 72
Subtracts fractions (6th) 74
Multiplies fractions (6th). 76
Divides fractions (6th) 78

Problem solving (story problems) (5th). 80

Geometry (5th). 82

MEASUREMENT
Understands time concepts (5th) 84
Understands area concept (5th) 86
Understands English system of length (5th). . . .88
Understands Metric system of length (5th) 90
Understands liquid and dry measurement (6th). . .92
Understands volume (6th). 94

Decimals (6th). 96

Percentage (6th). 98

Temperatures (F & C) (6th). 100

Experience with math lab (5th). . . . .

Evaluation: Self-Evaluative Method

1. Requires individual to develop personal standards based on personally identified needs. Each individual is master of her/his fate. Feedback may be solicited from expert facilitators and integrated into the self-evaluation.

2. Stresses internal motivation, based on personal satisfaction.

3. Requires no information. All feedback relates to "my development as a self-directed learner."

4. Receives feedback, self-evaluates, and reports as distinct processes controlled by the individual. If the learner chooses to enter a structured school, she/he will select that reporting device which will communicate her/his skills and knowledge effectively. In preparation, the self-directed learner may select a record-keeping system which will provide the information needed in the school application process.

5. Provides self-directed learning based on personally identified needs.

THE CENTER FOR SELF DIRECTED LEARNING

STUDENT EVALUATION OF COMPLETED LEARNING

STUDENT: David Abell

DATE: May 31

TITLE OF LEARNING: French

Describe the strong points of this learning experience, as well as those areas in which need more work. Give specific examples in each area.

I started this study late in the year (April), so I don't really feel qualified to do an evaluation. I think we have done a good job of reviewing in *French 2* as far as we have gotten, but I don't think I have learned much new material. My goals were not to learn new material, however, so I think this has been a successful experience in review for me. The reviewing has not been difficult for me since I retained much of what I learned in Parent School French last year, and it has really been a matter of refreshing my memory. Reading the Daudet stories has been delightful, and I have learned not only vocabulary and grammar, but Daudet's style and a sampling of French literature.

The sessions with Mrs. Manierre that I had were really great in both learning from the textbook and in reading the stories. Out of class, I wrote out exercises in *French 2* and Mrs. Manierre would check them over at our rendezvous. I think I could have moved faster through the textbook if I had set specific goals at the beginning such as doing two or three chapters a week. In this kind of work, it is possible to set more specific goals than in, say, Music Composition. Probably all I need to do is say what I'm going to do and then do it!

I enjoyed reading the Daudet stories the most, simply because I love the flowing sound of the language (of course I *do* understand it too), and I think my fluency in French has improved a lot since April. One thing I find easier now is reading a paragraph and getting the general meaning even if I don't understand half of the words. When I first started with Mrs. Manierre, I would have to go to the dictionary and look up alot of obscure words Daudet uses to get any meaning at all. Now I can read the paragraph through, get the general meaning (figuring out some of the words), and go back later to the dictionary.

Mrs. Manierre has really been a *partner* in this with me, refreshing her own memory along with me. I even had a head start on her because I have used *French 2* before. This got kind of awkward at times, but did make it more exciting; when we both didn't know something, we had to explore it together. But I do wish she would take on more of the role of teacher at times and question and drill me more. For example, I have trouble translating numbers into French and I would like it if she would drill me more on those.

THE CENTER	TEACHER'S EVALUATION OF COMPLETED LEARNING

STUDENT: David Abell   **TITLE OF LEARNING:** French

ADVISOR: Niebauer   **INDEPENDENT STUDY:** X

EVALUATOR: Mrs. Manierre   **DATE:** May 20

HOURS PER WEEK: 2   **NUMBER OF WEEKS:** 8

COMPLETED: X   **CONTINUING:**

EVALUATOR: Complete your evaluation after student has provided description, *return to the student after completion.*

In the weeks that I have been working with David in French, I have found him to be an exceptionally interested and highly motivated student. His foundation in grammar seems excellent, his vocabulary is good and his knowledge of verb forms and sentence structure seems unusually complete for someone who has had only two years of high school French. He must have retained just about everything he learned in those classes. His accent is good, and his enjoyment and appreciation of the French language, and the style of Alphonse Daudet whose stories we are reading, make it a real pleasure to work with him. He shows every sign of the likelihood of becoming very fluent and proficient in the language—in fact is so already. In some ways I feel he is at least as advanced a French scholar as I, and I hope that what we have done together has been as much help and pleasure to him as it has been to me!

REPORTING

Reporting options number like the stars: they come in all sizes, shapes, and colors. There is no single, magic way that will apply to every situation. Ideally, the reporting system will reflect what is best for each child within the reality frame of a changing society, the school's philosophy, and community pressures.

Reporting: Single Symbol

1. 5 Point Symbols

A	B	C	D	F
93	85	78	70	F
HP	P	MP	P	F
Excellent	Good	Average	Poor	Fail
90	80	70	60	F

Advantages

1. Distinguishes multiple levels of performance norms.
2. Most commonly used. Efficient record keeping provides grade-point averages. Col-

Disadvantages

1. Judgmental feedback.
2. More emphasis on efficient records than on specific, well-timed, usable feedback.
3. Motivates the A and B student, but dis-

lege admissions finds "most practical, and most reliable predictor of success."
3. Minimizes teacher record keeping.

courages all others and contributes to passive learners and dropouts.
4. Divides teachers and students.
5. Contributes to elitist, sexist, and racist divisions among students.
6. Creates a Watergate morality
7. Makes competition and grades more important than learning.

2. 4 Point Symbols/No Failure

A	B	C	Incomplete
HP	LP	P	NG
90	80	70	Incomplete
Excellent	Progress	Minimum Progress	

Advantages

1. Usable with all evaluation options but most compatible with criterion reference and self-evaluation. Reports only work completed or mastered.
2. Awards excellence but replaces failure concept with "no mastery" and avoids judgmental stigma. (Some argue "no failure" is a disadvantage. The assumption here is that schools should not exist to create stigmas, reinforce failure, or destroy self-images. Schools should help children learn how to succeed, not fail.)
3. Allows for a blend of evaluating-reporting methods. (A school individualizes instruction and wants its evaluation to reflect that philosophy. Parents demand grades. To compromise, this system is tied to a criterion checklist. Goal conferences are used to deal with each course and explain the system.)

Disadvantages

1. Allows parents, teachers, and students to misfocus. A grade, no matter what its shape, is a grade, especially when attention is not given to the school's reasons for devaluing grading.
2. Requires that teachers develop new methods which will help students focus on learning and self-motivation. (See William Glasser's *Schools Without Failure* for a detailed description of one approach valuable in helping children, teachers, and parents discover the joy of learning.)
3. Most colleges want all grades reported including failure. If used for final grades, this option would not meet that demand, and thus penalize the student applicant.

3. 2-3 Point Options/Failure

		P	F
		C	NC
		S	U
	HP	P	F
	Always	Sometimes	Never

Advantages

1. Usable with any evaluation option but most compatible with criterion reference and self-evaluation, especially when a symbol record is required by law or computer storage.
2. For those who insist upon a recorded F, it is provided.
3. Blends with the 5-point system to encourage course electives which will not figure into GPA. (Students may elect a P/F course without concern that the grade will enter into the GPA.)

Disadvantages

1. An either-or grade: success or failure. Provides a sharper focus on those who fail.
2. No allowance is made for changing the teaching-learning process. The external motivation of grades is taken away, but there is no guarantee that the teacher will introduce strategies to build internal motivation. Lacking also external motivation to learn, students choose the natural out.
3. Neither efficient nor effective. Pass/Fail gives colleges less information for selecting applicants, and gives no helpful feedback to students.

Reporting: Narrative Check Sheet

WINNETKA PUBLIC SCHOOLS
Winnetka, Illinois

REPORT OF PUPIL PROGRESS—INTERMEDIATE GRADE FORM I
CHILD'S NAME _____

MATHEMATICS

The math program is arranged in a developmental sequence. The Roman Numerals represent a series and should not be interpreted as grade level placement.

		DATE COMPLETED
MIXED OPERATIONS IV	Addition and substraction to four digits	
MULTIPLICATION III	Multiplication facts through product 81	
DIVISION III	Division facts through 81	
DIVISION IV	One digit divisors	
NUMERATION VI	Approximation of hundreds and thousands	
MULTIPLICATION IV	Three digit numbers multiplied by a one digit number	
MIXED OPERATIONS V	Addition and subtraction to six digits	
MULTIPLICATION V	Multiplication with two and three digit factors	
DIVISION V	Long division with two digit divisors	
NUMERATION VII	Approximation of thousands and millions	
FRACTIONS V	Addition and subtraction of unlike fractions	
FRACTIONS VI	Meaning of decimals	
MEASUREMENT VI	Linear measurement using metric system	
GEOMETRY V	Coordinate graphing	
MIXED OPERATIONS VI	Properties of the operations	
GEOMETRY VI	Types of lines	

	FALL	WINTER	SPRING
Reasons well in problem solving			
Works accurately			
Retains processes well			
Expected work completed			
Exhibits mastery of number facts			
Addition 3 minutes	75	80	85
Subtraction 3 minutes	70	75	80
Multiplication 3 minutes	70	75	80
Division 3 minutes	60	65	70

Advantages

1. Used with a criterion system, the checklist provides a practical, specific report of learning which allows students to take some responsibility for record keeping tasks.

2. Once organized, the checklists provide an efficient, individualized record of skills and concepts mastered in each subject area.

3. Combines easily with written reports, conferences, or "summative grades" to make an evaluation-feedback package that meets effective feedback criteria as well as providing efficient grades.

Disadvantages

1. When uncontrolled, sheer bulk created by multiple objectives, can inundate student and teacher with a mass of information. Record keeping time can gobble up the entire day.

2. Criterion checklists confuse parents who expect simple grade reports. Jargon, details, and unknown topics cause defensive reactions and bewilderment.

3. A well-constructed criterion report requires a detailed record system as backup. The creation of each classroom system requires special skills, time, and patience which the teacher does not have; maintainance demands even more attention.

4. Criterion reports communicate fragments of learning, seldom a whole picture.

5. Criterion reports concentrate on observable behaviors. Most teachers are not trained to distinguish the subtle differences which indicate a behavior change.

Reporting: Computer Printout

```
TEACHER COMMENT CATALOG FOR BEECHER SCHOOL DISTRICT          03/16/73

    CATEGORY 8000 - MUSIC

COMMENT NUMBER      *************      ASSOCIATED TEACHER COMMENT

    8011        IS WORKING UP TO GRADE LEVEL

    8021        IS WORKING BELOW GRADE LEVEL

    8031        IS WORKING ABOVE GRADE LEVEL

    8041        WILLINGLY PARTICIPATED IN ALL MUSICAL ACTIVITIES

    8051        NEEDS TO IMPROVE IN PARTICIPATING IN MUSIC CLASS

    8061        PARTICIPATED IN MUSIC CLASS

    8071        DOES NOT PARTICIPATE IN MUSIC CLASS

    8081        DEMONSTRATES INTEREST AND ENTHUSIAM IN SINGING

    8091        CREATES A DISTURBANCE DURING CLASS

    8101        DOES NOT PARTICIPATE IN SINGING ACTIVITIES

    8111        SINGS WELL AND CONTRIBUTES TO CLASS SINGING ACTIVITY

    8121        HAS A VERY NICE VOICE BUT DOES NOT USE IT

    8131        HAS DIFFICULTY MATCHING PITCHES

    8141        SHOWS LEADERSHIP ABILITY IN SINGING

    8151        LEADS CLASS IN SINGING ACTIVITY

    8161        SHOWS INTEREST IN LISTENING ACTIVITY
```

Reporting: Computer Printout (Continued)

8171	LISTENS DURING CLASS ACTIVITIES
8181	DOES NOT LISTEN DURING CLASS ACTIVITIES
8191	NEEDS TO IMPROVE IN CONCENTRATING ON LISTENING ACTIVITIES
8201	CONTRIBUTES TO LISTENING LESSONS DISCUSSIONS QUESTIONS
8211	NEEDS TO IMPROVE IN LISTENING LESSONS DISCUSSIONS QUESTIONS
8221	READS BASIC RHYTHMIC PATTERNS
8231	HAS DIFFICULTY IN READING BASIC RHYTHMIC PATTERNS
8241	RESPONDS TO BASIC RHYTHMIC PATTERNS
8251	HAS DIFFICULTY IN RESPONDING TO BASIC RHYTHMIC PATTERNS
8261	DEMONSTRATES LEADERSHIP IN RHYTHMIC ACTIVITY
8271	SHOWS INCREASING SKILL IN RHYTHMIC EXERCISES
8281	NEEDS IMPROVEMENT IN RHYTHMIC EXERCISES
8291	DEMONSTRATES GOOD RHYTHMIC ABILITY
8301	DEMONSTRATES INTEREST IN MUSICAL INSTRUMENTS
8311	HAS CONTRIBUTED TO MUSIC CLASS WITH THE USE OF INSTRUMENTS
8321	HAS INCREASED SKILL IN THE USE OF RHYTHM INSTRUMENTS
8331	SUGGEST INTERPRETIVE IDEAS IN MUSIC CLASS
8341	RECOGNIZES BASIC MUSICAL SYMBOLS EXAMPLE-TREBLE CLEF-SHARP-ETC

Advantages

1. Used with criterion system, the computerized report provides a practical, specific report of learning which allows students to select personal goals, individualized resource materials, and a personalized method of organization.

2. The computer printout allows for a flexible, continuous progress record adaptable for different levels in school. With minimum paperwork, one classroom teacher has access to criteria and feedback statements suitable for students working at any grade level in any skill or subject.

3. The computer printout, working from a centralized pool or bank of criteria and feedback statements, can generate as wide a range of statements—in a controlled language that meets effectiveness criteria—as needed by any teacher.

4. The computer printout combines easily with conferences or summative grades to make a helpful feedback package which meets effectiveness criteria as well as providing efficient grades.

5. The printout encourages instant, specific feedback with a minimum of teacher/student record keeping. Prepunched cards and cathode-ray touch screens replace long, involved checklists.

6. Thec computer printout encourages individualized selection of objectives for family goal-setting conferences. The family can select student goals from the masterlist. On the day the objective is reached, a printed card is automatically prepared and mailed by the computer. If the family wishes, the computer may add a grade to the report, as well as constructive suggestions for improvement.

Disadvantages

1. Computer printouts are unfamiliar territory. Some persons react emotionally to the computer printout's impersonal appearance. Others who expect simple grade reports are confused by the "abundance of cold information."

2. An efficient and effective printout system depends on the skill and mind set of the programmer. Just as the computer could only guarantee language which meets the feedback criteria, it could, at a programmer's behest, generate destructive feedback.

4. Criterion reports mechanically communicate learning by fragmented skills—the total is a sum of parts.

5. Cost and availability of skilled programmers is a major deterrent at this time.

6. A shortage of good software. Many states have developed "objective" banks, but few have developed criteria statements which when reported meet the feedback criteria. Long hours of staff time are needed to develop the software.

7. Requires a teacher skilled in helping students learn to set goals, select material, and keep accurate records. Such skills presuppose a high level of trust by the teacher.

8. Allows use of feedback statements which may not meet effectiveness criteria.

Reporting: Written Statement

LINN-MAR COMMUNITY SCHOOL DISTRICT

PROGRESS REPORT   19 __71__ - 19 __72__

Student   **Mary Smith** _____

Building _____

Grade Level ____4____

___**Mrs. Doe**_____   Teacher -

LEROY KRUSKOP, SUPERINTENDENT

Proper understanding between the home and the school is essential to effective guidance in the educational development of each child. It is felt a progress report of this nature will give parents a comprehensive view of their child's strengths and areas of needed improvement.

_____ Principal

Attendance by Periods			
	1st Sem.	2nd Sem.	Total
Days Present	85	88½	173½
Days Absent	4	2½	6½
Times Tardy	0	0	0

    Mary is a very capable student. Her work is usually well done.
Mary's only problem is her inability to control her temper and emotions.
Mary must learn to share and get along with others better. This year
Mary seems to have made much progress towards this. However, there are
still flares of temper tantrums and extreme emotional displays on Mary's

part. Mary needs to understand herself more. She needs a firm but
understanding hand.

Mary has made much progress in her reading class. She has been reading
and discovering good literature. She is making much better use of her
time and learning to work steadily. She has a good memory and diction.

Mary is showing much interest in Social Studies. She does her best
work in the written assignment area.

Mary has made good progress in Math and still needs to continue to
work on the multiplication and division factors.

Due to her temper Mary finds it difficult to work in small groups
without getting upset.

See Language insert.

Mary experienced great difficulty on the word usage pre-test. She
had trouble in the following five areas: saw-seen ate-eaten, went-gone,
did-don, and good-well. But much effort was put forth to correct her
mistakes. She did a numerous amount of practice sheets also. Mary's
effort was greatly repayed-her post test score was 122/123.

SECOND SEMESTER

Mary has tried hard in several social studies projects. Some
of her work shows good planning and research skills.

Her performance in reading has not been consistent this semester.
She put on a very well planned play and continues to show interests in
poetry. But her individualized reading has not progressed as well. Mary
seldom finishes a book she starts. Also she has much difficulty in
accepting constructive criticism.

Only one area of language gave Mary any difficulty. This was in
using correctly can and may. Usually she does quite well writing
creatively. She remembers how to use the basic rules of language
correctly. Mary is quite quick to pick up ideas so she seldom has any
real problems.

In Math, Mary has passed through the addition and subtraction facts
easily and is now working on the multiplication and division facts. She
made good progress through the math units this year.

Mary started in level 4 of spelling and is now working in level 17.
She has completed five levels since January and is making satisfactory
progress.

In science, the teachers felt Mary could have been more conscientious
in her written assignments. She completed most of the required work.
Here she could have gone into more depth and could have been neater.

PROMOTED TO FIFTH

Advantages

1. Can supplement a checklist, chart, or printout. Short, written statements can highlight a specific accomplishment, communicate a concern, or tie together the multiple fragments in a checklist so that parents can focus on overall progress as well as details. As a summation, the statement can clarify, point new directions, or ask questions.
2. Teaches each student to frame goals, negotiate expectations, and find resources appropriate to personal needs.
3. Encourages maximum interaction with teachers in seeking advice for each step in the learning process.
4. Allows comprehensive teacher feedback which not only meets the criteria for effective feedback, but also encourages individual examples and language personally directed to the student. Accomplishments are viewed in a wholistic perspective rather than as a series of isolated steps.
5. A transcript with written evaluations for each learning experience presents the most complete picture of an individual learner. Not only is there a list of course titles, but also descriptions of what and how the student learned, strengths and weaknesses, areas which need improvement, how time is used in relation to goals, resource use, and organization of learning.

Disadvantages

1. Can be a deadly, sarcastic weapon used to vent personal frustrations of evaluator.
2. Requires time, energy, and command of language. Good, written evaluations necessitate a thorough knowledge of each student, scheduled time blocks to allow teachers to write evaluations that meet feedback criteria, and good writing skills. Few teachers are given the time or the training to master the written evaluation.
3. Parents may not want to take the time to read a long evaluation.
4. The written evaluation produces more information than many admissions officers and business personnel directors want to read.

Reporting: Conferences

Sample forms from the Winnetka Public Schools for conducting a conference appear on pages 40-44.

Date_____ School _____

Parent's Name _____

Child's Name _____

Teacher _____ Grade _____

PLEASE
BRING THIS FORM
TO YOUR
SCHEDULED
CONFERENCE.
IT WILL BE YOUR
RECORD.

WINNETKA PUBLIC SCHOOLS
CONFERENCE GUIDE AND RECORD FOR PARENTS AND TEACHERS
Grades III to VIII

We are sending this combination guide and record as a convenience for you in looking forward to our conference. We urge you to go over the following pages carefully to see how you can contribute to our conference and to be informed concerning areas of progress your child's teacher will be evaluating.

Your conference is scheduled for_____ at_____ o'clock

in_____.

Sincerely yours,

COOPERATIVE ACTION AGREED UPON IN OUR CONFERENCE

_____to continue present program unchanged

_____to pursue the following plan: (date each agreement separately as developed during the year)

You are invited to select from the following topics those that seem important to you in helping us to understand your child better. A space is provided for you to record essential information for use during the conference and for subsequent reference immediately after the conference.

TOPICS	PARENTS' NOTES Before and after conference
1. What is your child's reaction to school?	
2. What are his out-of-school activities?	
3. What are his special interests?	
4. Does he have some regular responsibilities at home?	
5. How does he react to authority and control? Is he developing self-discipline?	
6. Is he developing good health habits?	
7. Does he have some physical difficulty we should know about?	
8. Are there other things we should know about your child?	

WINNETKA PUBLIC SCHOOLS
Winnetka, Illinois

CHILD'S NAME _____

	FALL			WINTER			SPRING		
	Usually	Sometimes	Seldom	Usually	Sometimes	Seldom	Usually	Sometimes	Seldom

WORK HABITS:

Listens with attention									
Works steadily at a task									
Checks work carefully									
Works independently									
Uses time wisely									
Follows directions									
Strives to improve work									
Works in neat and orderly manner									
Takes care of materials and property									
Completes assignment in reasonable time									
Shows initiative									

PERSONAL DEVELOPMENT

Gets along well with others									
Works well in a small group									
Works well in a large group									
Respects the rights of others									
Shows willingness to serve									
Assumes responsibility									
Uses self-control									
Follows school regulations									

Days absent _____   Parent's signature _____
                Fall   Fall

           _____   _____
                Winter   Winter

           _____
                Spring

WINNETKA PUBLIC SCHOOLS
Winnetka, Illinois

REPORT OF PUPIL PROGRESS — INTERMEDIATE GRADE FORM

CHILD'S NAME _____

LANGUAGE ARTS

TEACHER'S NAME _____

Language Arts is a spiral curriculum. Concepts are introduced at specific grade levels. It is understood that the same concept will be studied again later in the year or in the future years in greater depth. Therefore, when a child receives an Acceptable Progress evaluation it means he has sufficiently mastered the material studied at that time. Parents may assume that if a space has been left blank, the material will be covered at a later date.

	FALL			WINTER			SPRING		
	Acceptable Progress	More Progress Needed		Acceptable Progress	More Progress Needed		Acceptable Progress	More Progress Needed	
READING									
Reads with understanding, as evidenced by:									
Participation in discussion									
Completion of reading assignments									
Meets book report requirements									
Reads well orally									
SPELLING									
Spells assigned words correctly									
Spells correctly in written work									
STUDY SKILLS									
Develops note-taking for gathering information									
Organizes ideas									
Uses a variety of resources									
Uses reference materials and the Resource Center									
HANDWRITING									
Formation of letters (uniformity of size, shape, slant, spacing)									
General appearance of all work									
PRACTICE EXERCISES FOR LANGUAGE SKILLS									
Punctuation, capital letters, etc.									
Grammar									
Dictionary usage									
WRITTEN EXPRESSION									
Application of punctuation, capital letters, etc.									
Sentence structure									
Paragraph structure									
Development of ideas									
ORAL EXPRESSION									

WINNETKA PUBLIC SCHOOLS
Winnetka, Illinois

REPORT OF PUPIL PROGRESS — INTERMEDIATE GRADE FORM I

CHILD'S NAME _____

SCIENCE

The units of study in science utilize the student's interest in a variety of phenomena in the environment as motivation for laboratory experiences. Students are expected to utilize observation, classification, recording and data collecting to answer the questions raised in the units. The science program consists of one semester of Energy Sources and one on the Systems of the Human Body.

	FALL			WINTER			SPRING		
	Acceptable	Progress is More Progress	Needed	Acceptable	Progress is More Progress	Needed	Acceptable	Progress is More Progress	Needed
Manipulates and uses equipment carefully and accurately									
Makes careful observations									
Records information and communicates findings									
Retains concepts developed in the unit									
Cleans up equipment independently									

Units include:
    Energy Sources
    Human Body Systems
        Skeletal
        Muscular
        Senses
        Digestive
        Reproductive

SOCIAL STUDIES

The fifth grade Social Studies program consists primarily of Man: A Course of Study. The content of the course is man: his nature as a species, the forces that shaped and continue to shape his humanity. Three questions recur throughout: What is human about human beings? How did they get that way? How can they be made more so?

In addidition, study may include units related to the United States such as Vikings, Exploration, Colonization, Indians, Western Expansion, Geography, Map Skills, and Current Events.

	FALL			WINTER			SPRING		
	Acceptable	Progress is More Progress	Needed	Acceptable	Progress is More Progress	Needed	Acceptable	Progress is More Progress	Needed
Reads and interprets maps and map legends									
Participates thoughtfully in group discussions									
Contributes toward group projects									
Shows satisfactory understanding and retention of material studied									

COMMENTS:

Advantages

1. Used in combination with any other evaluating-reporting method, the conference adds a personal dimension impossible to achieve with the printed form.

2. The conference is the most easily implemented change. When a community will not surrender traditional grades, the conference, used as a family goal-setting strategy (see page 47), can reduce the negative consequences of grades, and focus student-parent attention on more positive aspects of the teaching-learning process. In the conference, the teacher can provide constructive feedback and help each family remedy each child's learning difficulties.

3. When used in a family, goal-setting context, additional advantages accrue to teachers, parents, and students:

    a. Learning as codefined by the family and the teacher increases the parents' sense of belonging in the school and control of the child's learning. As the parents feel more involved in the school, they will more readily take an active role in contributing time and expertise in helping the child learn and in volunteering service to the school.

    b. The conference teacher's feedback techniques give parents new options and skills in helping the child take responsibility for specific, goal-formed learning, based on his/her needs.

    c. The conference builds the self-concept of the child who discovers helpful resources and new ways to be self-accountable for learning.

    d. School-family cooperation, trust, and responsibility for the child's learning are encouraged.

    e. Teachers and parents are motivated to communicate clearly and openly their expectations of the child and his/her learning.

    f. The conference helps the family clarify their values on what and how learning should occur for their child.

    g. Each family is drawn into an active, supportive, and meaningful role in the education of their children.

    h. Self-evaluation is encouraged based on personal, specific, nonjudgmental, and criteria-referenced evaluation and reporting procedures appropriate to each child's needs.

    i. Teachers gain new perspectives on each child's needs.

    j. The conference reports realistically and accurately what each child has learned. Effective feedback, not efficiency, is given top priority.

Disadvantages

1. Adequate conferences require time—time for preparation by the teacher and the parent and time to conduct a thorough conference based on effective feedback techniques. If the conference is a PR gimmick, or a five-minute "Hello, I'm Mrs. Smith. Julie is a lovely student," it has no real value as an effective reporting or goal-setting device.

2. Parents, long excluded from meaningful participation in the schools, or recalling old conference methods, will not take to the idea of a 30-minute conference. More planning time will be required for the staff, administration, and parent leaders to devise strategies that will attract parents to the goal-setting conference.

3. Teachers, who have perceived conferences as a PTA agenda which encroaches on their time, will object to half-hour conferences as an infringement on the already too short time to teach. Attitudes must change to see the conference as a tool which will improve learning.

4. Most teachers do not have the training they may feel is necessary to conduct a goal-setting conference. How do I prepare? How do I involve the parents? What are my limits? These are all legitimate questions which will require in-service assistance.

k. Evaluation feedback is made a key component in the teaching-learning process. Learning is communicated as a growth cycle, not a list of accomplishments or a pile of starred projects.
l. The conference helps teachers and parents see the unique WHOLE child, learning and growing with their support and expertise. When planning goals and strategies for learning, they consider all the needs which may influence how, what, and why the child learns, what problems inhibit learning, and how self-discipline can be developed.

If the teachers and parents in a school insist that day-to-day feedback meet the effectiveness criteria, then the district can more easily balance the children's developmental needs with parent needs for traditional grades and institutional demands for efficient records. Ideally, each evaluation given to a student would meet all criteria fully. In reaching for the ideal, some compromises that, hopefully, are to the students' benefit, must be made.

The most satisfactory compromises are an amalgam of reporting methods which maintain the best possible balance between specific, informative, non-judgmental, and criterion-referenced reports and an amount of paper that does not overwhelm parents or teachers.

THE GOAL-SETTING CONFERENCE: "TEACHER, MEET MY PARENTS."

At one time, the family was the center of learning. As cities grew into urban monsters and society became a technological complex, the responsibility for teaching and learning was taken from the family and given to school professionals. As family roles specialized, the demands of work superseded time for parents and children (those who weren't in the factories) to discuss school. A quarterly report card, glanced over quickly, was the extent of parent involvement.

Today, as leisure time and the importance of learning increase, parent concern about quality education has mounted. Schooling has evolved into a major preoccupation that causes open conflict about method, content, discipline, and value systems. Confused and alienated, families try to reassert control over their children's learning by attacking school board policies on discipline, textbook selection, and curriculum, by voting down tax referenda needed to finance teacher raises, and by making scapegoats of busing and attendance policies. In the last five years, parents have more directly confronted school professionals with demands for decision-making control than at any time in this century.

While many school districts have responded defensively, others have demonstrated that parent involvement can benefit the school and the community.

- Multiple Alternatives, as in Southeast Minneapolis, Berkeley, Portland, Quincy, and Wayne County, Michigan.

- Alternative Schools as in Ann Arbor's Earth Works, New York's Mini-Schools, Grand Rapids' Street Academy, St. Louis' Metro High, St. Paul's Open School, and Dallas' Skyline Career Academy.

- Schools-within-Schools as in Indianapolis' North Central High, Park Forest's Rich East High, San Mateo High, Garden City, Kansas, and Wisconsin Rapids.

- Family Goal-Setting Conferences as in Mt. Lake, Minnesota, Milwaukee, Wisconsin, and Winnetka, Illinois.

- Parent Councils as in Evanston's King Lab School, North St. Paul's Middle School, and Concord, California's Weathervane School.

The most practical device to bring parents into the school decision-making process is to begin with the parents' concern for their children's academic progress. Although it requires detailed planning, the family goal-setting conference not only involves parents, it gives them a direct voice in *what* and *how* each child learns. Most importantly, however, when used for goal setting, evaluating, and reporting, the family conference adds the personal, family-oriented dimension which most contemporary schooling lacks.

In initiating the family goal conference as an integral part of the school program, a district announces that it views education as the joint responsibility of the parents, the teacher, and the child. The value of such responsibility is learned, however, not merely by the announcement, but most effectively by the opportunity to be involved in those decisions for which the individual—teacher, parent, or student—is being held accountable.

The essence of the goal-setting family conference is communication and support. When the child is learning to assume greater responsibility for learning, the support and expertise of concerned adults with different, but helpful viewpoints are needed. The family conference, which relies on effective feedback techniques, provides an ideal setting in which the child can receive this support and guidance. By communicating openly, parents and teachers avoid the crossed and conflicting messages which confuse the child.

To initiate the family conference, a committee of parents and teachers should plan how to implement the practice. In addition to planning objectives, responsibilities, and procedures, the committee must identify possible obstacles that might hinder successful implementation, decide on the resources that will help and the strategies necessary to insure success.

Step 1. Forming the Objectives of the Family Conference

Each school will draw up its own list of objectives. In general, however, there are six major goals for the family conference:

1. To help parents and teachers interpret together the school's educational program in terms of goals attuned to each child's needs.

2. To help each family set learning goals for each child.

3. To provide ways and means for the parents and teachers to help

4. To encourage the child to assume greater responsibility for setting goals, selecting resources and materials, organizing and evaluating her/his learning.

5. To appraise together the child's growth and academic progress according to mutually set criteria based on the child's needs.

6. To establish strong lines of communication among parents, student, and teacher.

Step 2. Identifying Responsibilities

1. *Scheduling.* The principal should schedule at least two conferences, 20 to 30 minutes long, each year, during school days. The conference days and times should be convenient to parents, but not an additional burden to teachers. Some options might be:

- If the number of single parent or working parent families is low, schedule conference periods during regular school days. Reserve several early morning, late afternoon, or evening times for the working parents. Scatter the reserved times over several weeks.

- If working parents are a large number, schedule conference days to begin in mid-afternoon. Half of the staff will conduct school at the regular time for all students. (Large group presentations, field trips, and mini-courses with community and parent volunteers, a feature film, or an assembly program can be planned.) The other half will prepare and conduct the conferences. On a second day, the staff will reverse tasks. (This arrangement has several advantages: it varies the student program, allows for cooperative staff planning, gives an opportunity for new learning experiences and experimental programming, intensifies community involvement, and allows time for conference planning by staff.)

- Start the conference days at 2 p.m. Count each conference day as a school day. Students come to school only for the conference.

- End the school day one hour early on one day each week. Each teacher might schedule three to five conferences in those times.

- End the school day two hours early twice monthly. Parents, students, and teachers return for scheduled evening conferences and other activities. Additional conferences, phone conversations, or written notes may be initiated by parents or teachers.

2. *Staff Development.* The administration is responsible for scheduling staff development workshops. A teacher committee should plan the program so that each teacher understands the why and how of the conference and develops the techniques that will insure an effective conference. By using role playing, structured lab experiences, and small group counseling exercises, teachers should learn:

- How to set realistic, achievable, and personal goals which meet their own needs as teachers.

- How to prepare for each conference.

- How to accept nonjudgmentally, without surprise or disapproval, what the child or parent may say in a conference.

- How to begin and end the conference with positive comments about the child's progress and behavior.

- How to help the parent and child clarify and accept what the child enjoys in school, what the child fears or dislikes about school, how the child works best (small group, independent study, or other), what improvements are needed, the child's strong skills, how the teacher or parents can help each other and the child, and new directions for the child's learning.

- How to arrange chair groupings which will open communication.

- How to offer alternative solutions so that the family may decide how to solve a problem.

- How to listen actively.

- How to discern the perceptions behind statements.

- How to help parents and child to listen nonjudgmentally.

- How to provide effective feedback.

- How to interpret information the school has about the child and that the parents may want or that is relevant to the conference, such as—
  a. recorded observations of pupil performance as shown by class involvement, written work, group activities, and behavior.
  b. dated samples of the student's work.
  c. all tests: informal quizzes, teacher-made unit tests, pre- and post-unit tests, standardized achievement and aptitude tests.
  d. summaries of past conferences as contained in the cumulative record.
  e. health records.

3.   *Parent Preparation.* School goals, conference procedures and responsibilities, and methods to make parents aware of conference dates can be the responsibility of the PTA. The PTA can involve many parents in a phone campaign, run ads in the local newspaper, send letters, hold informal talks or teas about the conference plans, or run a door-to-door survey. As a final preparation, the conference planners should provide each family with a guidebook that outlines and explains the what, why, and how of the school's evaluation-reporting conference, and a Fall Conference Planning Sheet for parents.

Dear Parent:

In order to help all of us benefit from the upcoming conference on

_____ , I am requesting that each of us complete the

questions outlined below.

Thank you.

Simon Jones

PARENT CONFERENCE PLANNING

Instruction I: Unless your child is new to this school, begin by reviewing the summary of last spring's conference. Discuss the summary with your child.

Instruction II: Answer the following questions. (Your child and I have already completed a similar questionnaire.)

1. What are your concerns for this child in school this year?
2. What does your child most need to improve? (As a guide, check the curriculum guidebook you received when your child registered in the school.)
3. How much improvement do you expect this year?
4. If you were to select two "needs to improve" for your child, which would you choose?
5. List some ways you think the school might best help your child meet these needs?
6. List some ways in which you might help.

Instruction III: After completing the questionnaire, discuss the responses with your child. Listen for her/his reactions. What are the areas of agreement? Disagreement?

Instruction IV: Bring your answers to the family conference. Together, we will discuss your child's needs and help her/him set goals for the year. Because of the half-hour time limit for your conference, it is important that each of us come prepared. You have a right to know all the school knows about your child. I will interpret that information for the benefit of your child's education.

The open-ended questions in the above planning form may disconcert some parents who need more specific guidelines. For those parents the form on pages 51 and 52 is more helpful.

Dear Parent:

In order that the conference regarding your child's program can benefit all of us, I am asking that you prepare for the conference by completing this questionnaire. Bring your responses to the conference.

Sincerely,

Mary Thomas

CONFERENCE PREPARATION FOR PARENTS

Instruction I: Think about your child as you answer these questions. In each section, give a (1) to the question which is most important to you, a (2) to the second most important, and so on.

(A) I need information about my child's academic progress.

____ What is my child's capacity for learning and how does her/his work compare with that ability?

____ What specifically should my child learn in school? (Refer to the curriculum guide. List your priorities.)

____ In what ways has my child's work improved or slipped since the last conference?

____ (Other)

(B) I need information on how my child learns.

____ Does my child know how to set goals that she/he accomplishes?

____ Does my child use "unplanned" time wisely?

____ Does my child learn better in large groups, seminars, or independent work?

____ Can my child apply new learning to new situations?

____ What problem-solving skills does my child use?

____ (Other)

(C) I need information on my child's self-direction.

____ Can my child identify her/his learning needs?

____ Can my child set realistic long- and short-range goals?

____ Can my child hear and follow directions?

____ Can my child select and use a variety of learning materials?

____ Can my child set and meet priorities?

____ Can my child assess or evaluate her/his work?

____ Can my child act independently of peer pressure?

____ (Other)

(D)   I need information on my child's peer relationships.

_____   Does my child offer to help others?

_____   Does my child respect others' property?

_____   Does my child live up to peer commitments?

_____   Does my child share responsibility?

_____   Is my child sensitive to her/his peers' feelings?

_____   Does my child respect differences of values among her/his peers?

_____   (Other)

(E)   I need information on my child's creative work.

_____   Does my child use a variety of media to express herself/himself?

_____   Does my child concentrate on creative work?

_____   Does my child use creative talents

_____   (Other)

Instruction II. The following is a summary list of the five categories. Rank each category according to its importance to you.

_____I need information on my child's academic progress.

_____I need information on how my child learns.

_____I need information on my child's self-direction.

_____I need information on my child's peer relationships.

_____I need information on my child's creative work.

_____(Other)

Instruction III. Take your no. 1 choice from Instruction II. Frame questions which identify your major concerns in that category. Continue through each of your categories and write down the most important questions.

What I am most concerned about in category 1 is _____

_____

_____

_____

What I most want to know is _____

_____

_____

Bring your questions to the conference.

Thank you.

4. *Teacher Responsibilities.* The teacher will prepare for the conference by using the same questionnaire as the parents. In addition she/he will direct the student to gather test papers, projects, folders, and notes and will help the student complete the questionnaire. At conference time, the teacher initiates the discussion by reviewing conference procedures, by making sure that parents and child understand the procedures, and by sharing her/his expectations for the conference: (1) that each person will listen actively to the individual speaking and respect that person's point of view; (2) that each person will respond with respectful tones of voice; (3) that the group will focus on common concerns, and work together to solve problems; (4) that each person will openly share her/his concerns and needs.

After the teacher has clarified these expectations and set the conference tone, child and parents should express their respective expectations.

Kindergarten and primary students should receive help in framing and communicating ideas. Older children, if given the experience in the early grades, will have more facility in the task. Carefully worded questions will facilitate the child's contribution. Supportive and clarifying adult responses will encourage the child's involvement.

As the second step, the participants should share concerns, ask questions, and discuss the questionnaires. The teacher will assist in this step and ensure that each family member has the opportunity to speak. After 10 or 12 minutes, the teacher should clarify the major concerns expressed, and help the family synthesize the priority issues into clear problem statements. As a final step, the family frame learning-goal statements.

In follow-up conferences, the procedure will vary. Some families may seek more specific assistance in solving problems that have arisen during the school year. Rather than give answers, the teacher should suggest alternative solutions and help the family select the most appropriate for its needs. Other families may wish to focus on progress toward the student's goals. The teacher will make available materials showing the student's progress. No matter what the focus of a follow-up conference, the teacher should make certain that new goals are established.

In closing the conference the teacher has three tasks. First, she/he will write a goal contract *with* the family. The contract will list major goals, outline a plan of action, and describe responsibilities.

The second teacher responsibility in closing the conference is the recording task. The teacher will see that the contract with goals and responsibilities is written out and that copies are made for the family and for the student's file.

Finally, the teacher will facilitate concluding comments from each person. Tag statements such as "I'm pleased that". . ."In the conference, I appreciated. . ." made first by the teacher, will provide the necessary termination.

When used in conjunction with a traditional grade report or a criterion-based report, the semester goal conferences should include a review of progress, feedback to ensure a full understanding by student and parents of the criteria completed, and suggestions for improvement. For elementary school students, the single conference poses few scheduling problems. For departmentalized junior high and secondary school students, however, multiple teachers complicate the conference scheduling process. The most successful methods incorporate an advisor system in which one faculty member acts as coordinator in a fifteen to twenty-minute goal conference based on information gathered from the other teachers. Parents who wish more in-depth discussion with individual subject matter teachers are scheduled by the advisor to confer with those teachers. So that parents will not misuse this opportunity, all problems are first discussed with the advisor. Only those problems which the advisor cannot successfully facilitate are referred to the teachers.

(Shubert School Goal Contract)

Name _____Jordi Jones_____ Teacher _____Mary Todd_____

Date _____Sept. 27_____ Grade_____3_____

Jordi will concentrate on improvement in the following areas:

a. checking his work for accuracy

b. following directions

c. understanding and using place value (math)

d. expressing self so that he can be understood (oral)

e. understanding and practicing care of self

f. drawing conclusions from direct observation (science)

g. enjoying reading independently.

Report date: December 15

Mrs. Todd will provide materials for Jordi's work with c, d, and f. Jordi will pick four to six library books and self-schedule 40 minutes of classroom reading time each day. Jordi will maintain present performance levels in all other subject areas. Mr. Jones will help Jordi make a personal care checklist and review Jordi's personal care habits each night. Mrs. Jones will review Jordi's home study for a and b each night.

J. J.
M. J.
M. T.

---

5. *Student Responsibilities.* The student has three responsibilities for the goal conferences:

1. To prepare her/his own responses to the questionnaire.
2. To collect all materials relevant to the conference (tests, reports, projects, workbooks, etc.).
3. To participate in evaluating her/his learning and in setting goals.

Step 3. Evaluating the Goal-Setting Conference

Every evaluation-reporting system needs continual scrutiny. A district that uses the goal-setting conference should establish a parent-teacher-administrator-student (junior high and senior high) review committee. The committee's responsibility is to establish criteria for evaluating, methods for assessing, and strategies for improving the system. This committee may also serve as the steering group which sets conference dates, handles scheduling details, suggests in-service programs, and makes possible other parent involvement in activities such as a newsletter, parent-class nights, and student-parent fun nights.

CHANGING THE SYSTEM: MAKING CHANGE WITH YOUR NICKEL

The National Center for Grading/Learning Alternatives
811 Foxdale
Winnetka, Illinois 60093

Dear Educator:

We are a small, rural high school. Some of our faculty and parents are unhappy with our grading. We use the ABCDF. We would like to change our report card. We are thinking about a Pass-Fail system or an A-B-C-D and C-N/C. Last year two classes experimented with written evaluations. One teacher loved the personal approach; the other lamented the time involved. The Board of Education has instructed me to propose a solution, before the end of this school year. I have read *Wad-Ja-Get?* And I believe that we need to change. Can you tell me what system works best?

Sincerely,

Samuel Hill
Principal

Dr. Hill's letter pinpoints the difficulty a school faces when dissatisfaction with grades surfaces. It also demonstrates several of the unhelpful assumptions about the change process, such as:

Some faculty and parents are unhappy
to *change* our *report card*
considering *reporting* alternatives
two classes *experimented;* one *liked,* one *disliked*
I have read and *I* believe
solution *by end of year*
what system works best?

In order that an institutional change may benefit the people for whom it is intended, rather than merely promote efficiency, that change requires careful planning, great patience, firm conviction, and a complete understanding of the ingredients necessary for successful, effective change. Dr. Hill's misstatements indicated that his attempts to change the grading system would end in frustration. A more rational approach would have been to examine the criteria for effective change.

1.   *Change is effective when it encompasses the needs of all persons it will affect.* Dr. Hill indicated "*some* parents and teachers" were unhappy with traditional grades. Subsequent correspondence revealed that Dr. Hill had reacted to this dissatisfaction in terms of his own predispositions against grades. He had not attempted to check out how parents and other faculty felt, or to raise their understanding of the issues. In addition, his request for "the best system," a universal cure-all, avoided consideration of the community's needs and the criteria for effective evaluation.

2.   *Change is effective when it is based on a clear set of priorities.* Dr. Hill discussed the various options for changing the report card *symbols*. He had not considered the consequences of those seemingly minute adjustments. Other than meeting some parent and student dissatisfaction, the thrust for change bore no relation to the school's teaching-learning process.

3.   *Changes is effective when the persons affected are involved in the decision-making process.* Dr. Hill and the school board were making the decisions: a new system by the end of the school year. Although this is the traditional practice of school bureaucracies in making decisions, it indicates why relations among parents, teachers, administrators, and school boards are so poor; exclusion from decision making leads to alienation, noninvolvement, and mistrust. In this context the status quo, most blatantly represented by traditional grades, is the safe and secure stance. No matter what system Dr. Hill and the board might implement, it would have some community opposition. Following the usual path, the board would perceive the opposition as directed against the grading change and not as consequent on their failure to include teachers and parents in the decision-making process.

4.   *Change is effective when it is a planned process.* Viewed in a problem-solving perspective, effective change requires realistic goal setting based upon a clearly defined institutional need, examination of helpful resources, identification of possible obstacles, optional strategies, detailed organization, and evaluation against pre-established criteria. When these steps are not followed, change becomes haphazard, a search for a magic cure-all. Change, as a process, is a continual effort to improve a system, not the sudden emergence of a perfect product. In this sense, Dr. Hill's hope for a "best grading system" is an impossible dream.

In the years since the First National Conference on Grading Alternatives, change theory, applied to the reformation of evaluating and reporting methods, has evolved clear patterns for effective evaluation and reporting systems based on these criteria. Many school districts start the change effort by focusing on the reporting system's numbers and letters, just as Dr. Hill did. This is a false start. Essentially, the traditional reporting system is NOT the problem. Grades are only a part of the problem. Traditional grades reflect an outmoded learning theory which perceives motivation in limited stimulus-response terms. In practice, the Thorndyke model has evolved into "carrots" and "sticks," rewards and punishments, which should motivate ALL students to become disciplined learners; instead, it fosters apathy, increased discipline problems, disenchantment, and dropping out.

A newspaper story recently reported a local board of education meeting at which four inner city high school students described conditions in their school. The problems included cheating, teacher apathy, vandalism, and lax security.

Lack of discipline gave rein to cheating and to disruptive students. Teachers gossiped and did not bother at times even to attend classes. Lockers were broken into and property stolen. The so-called security system made it possible for almost anyone to obtain an I.D. card.

One board member pronounced the situation to be far more than a security problem. A fundamental attitudinal change is needed, she said.

To correct the misfocus caused by grades, a school district must decide *what is important*. The Forest Road School in La Grange Park, Illinois, developed a series of faculty-parent seminars and questionnaires to discover real classroom priorities. The final report listed the following:

At Forest Road, we believe that every student should learn—

1. To treat other persons with respect.
2. To contribute to each other's learning.
3. To express ideas and feelings clearly.
4. To feel good about herself/himself.
5. To take responsibility and independence as a learner.
6. To develop skills in each subject area appropriate to her/his ability.

A second Forest Road decision asked that evaluation and reporting reinforce the community's classroom priorities, yet allow for individual differences. A faculty-parent committee developed these guidelines:

Our evaluation should—

1. Measure individual effective growth by means of consistent criteria.
   a. respect for others
   b. contributions to others
   c. communication of ideas and feelings
   d. development of positive self-image
   e. responsibility
   f. independence
2. Measure individual effective learning by consistent criteria at each grade level.

Our reporting should—

1. Communicate individual affective and cognitive growth in relation to criteria.
   a. establishment of continuum for affective growth
   b. development consistent mastery levels in cognitive skills
2. Combine a variety of *manageable* reporting devices.
   a. student-kept records
   b. checklists/continuums
   c. three conferences yearly with released time and based on parent goals
   d. positive and constructive tone

As a third step, faculty committees, using the criteria for effective feedback, developed sequenced skills for each subject area.

Language Arts Skills
(levels 4-5-6)

I. Composition

Maintains skills learned in previous grades

Writes four types of sentences correctly in sequentially developed accounts

Writes paragraphs around a topic sentence

Develops a story using opening, plot, and closing

Retells myths, fables, folktales in characteristic literary form

Prepares and presents oral reports selecting vocabulary, construction, and diction appropriate to purpose and audience

Cooperates in discussions by responding as well as listening.

II. Sentences

Identifies and uses four sentence types

Changes nonsentences into sentences

Changes word order to improve meaning

Organizes notes for a short, summary report

Recognizes nouns, verbs, descriptive words, subjects, and predicates

Uses direct and indirect address in sentences.

III. Capitalization

Maintains skills of earlier grades

Uses capitals consistently for first word of sentence, to introduce direct quotations, for proper names, for personal pronouns.

IV. Punctuation

Uses period after all statements, in outlines, abbreviations

Uses quotation marks correctly

Uses commas to separate words in series, set off words in direct address

Recognizes and uses quotation marks

Uses apostrophes in contractions, singular possessive nouns

Uses underlining for book titles.

V. Handwriting

Writes legibly and neatly in all written work

Uses consistent slant

Has uniform size and shape of letters and numerals

Proofreads and corrects trouble spots

Practices improvement in all subject areas.

As the Forest Road committees developed the evaluation and reporting devices, a number of new problems emerged. Each problem was resolved as a "need response."

Problem	Solution Devised
1. Need for individualized materials which spanned several grade levels in each classroom 2. Need for record system which children could use 3. Need for classroom aides to help in distribution of materials, tutoring and other small tasks 4. Need to help students develop effective skills 5. Need for greater variety of individualized materials.	1. Redistribution of materials among grades so that each classroom had a range of levels in the materials (for example, in grade 3, the classroom would have materials for grades 1-5) 2. Development of a single mimeographed booklet with the K-7 skill sequence for each subject area. As a child completed a posttest, she/he made an X and entered date 3. Establishment of a parent-volunteer pool, and a cross-age tutoring program 4. Expansion of magic circle to daily use, K-4. Implemented advisory time in upper grades with special materials to develop the desired skills 5. Establishment of administrator-faculty review committee. Summer stipend to seek out and adapt materials from other schools, publishers.

In the problem-solving context, Forest Road worked four years to bring its learning program into agreement with its objectives. The problems of conference planning time, scheduling, and the checklists which reported public progress became a mechancial task, because the committees had so carefully laid the necessary "process" groundwork and had gone through the process, step-by-step. Today, their process continues as Forest Road attempts to "clean" its reporting system so that it will reflect the effectiveness criteria as closely as possible.

Getting Started

First steps are hardest. In dealing with the grading issue, it is rash to plunge headlong into battle. To introduce the grading issue without inducing heavy emotional reactions, identify parents and teachers who have similar views. Here are some practical strategies:

● Have lunch with a different teacher every day. Discuss the students, the teacher's views on cheating, competition, apathy. Spend your time listening. Encourage your meal partner to discuss each issue thoroughly. "Can you say more about that?" "Could you explain?"
● Purchase a basic library of grading materials. Xerox chapters and articles for faculty mail boxes, departmental offices, the school board.

Suggested Reading

Sidney Simon, Howard Kirschenbaum, Rodney Napier. *Wad-Ja-Get? The Grading Game in American Education.* New York: Hart Publishing Co., Inc., 1971.

The basic antigrades text. Written as part fiction, it covers the issues, the research, and the alternatives. In addition, an excellent appendix reviews the major research on grading.

William Glasser, "The Effect of School Failure on the Life of A Child." Washington, D.C.: National Association of Elementary Schools Principals, 1971.

A reprint of a two-part article published in the September and November, 1969, issues of *The National Elementary Principal.* This excellent article goes directly to the heart of the failure-success issue. It describes succinctly how most school problems, including apathy and anger, are caused by the failure syndrome. A basic book for grading reform.

William Glasser, *Schools Without Failure.* New York: Harper and Row, 1969.

An extended version of Glasser's article on failure. This book expands the discussion to include "how to" build success schools based on positive self-esteem.

Sidney Simon and James Bellanca, editors. *Degrading the Grading Myths: A Primer of Alternatives to Grades and Marks.* Washington, D.C.: Association for Supervision and Curriculum Development, 1976.

A collection of essays, including articles by Combs, Napier, Kirschenbaum, and more than a dozen other "change agents" who successfully pioneered grading reform, is built around four subtopics: the issues, the alternatives, the change process, and the results. A basic book for grading reform.

Howard Kirschenbaum and James Bellanca, *College Guide for Experimenting High Schools.* Upper Jay, New York: National Humanistic Education Center, 1973.

The *Guide* is a resource book for high schools, which shows in black and white that colleges do accept nontraditional high school transcripts. The exact requirements for 2,700 colleges are described in response to the question, "If no grades, what must a transcript contain?"

Benjamin Bloom, J. Thomas Hastings, and George F. Madaus. *Handbook on Formative and Summative Evaluation of Student Learning.* New York: McGraw-Hill Book Co., 1971.

The basic text for those who wish to create a competency criterion-based evaluation system. Very thorough research reports are included.

● At a faculty meeting, break into small groups. In each group, listen to taped speeches about grades. (Arthur Combs, "Grading and What We Know About Learning" (Upper Jay, New York: National Humanistic Education Center, 1973); Sidney Simon, "A Personal Search for a Grade" (National Humanistic Education Center, 1973); Howard Kirschenbaum, "Alternative Approaches to Grades" (National Humanistic Education Center, 1973); Rodney Napier, "The Change Agent and Grading Reform" (National Humanistic Education Center, 1973))

- Ask your students to discuss grades.
- Invite a speaker to address the PTA about evaluating and reporting. Use *The Grading Game* to open the discussion.
- Plan a faculty in-service day. Divide the faculty into subgroups and use any of the following surveys to open the conversation. Ask each subgroup to report to the whole faculty at the end of the in-service day. Give guidelines for the reports.
- Distribute Data Feedback Questionnaires:

Instruction: Within each section, rank the seven statements.

Reporting

_____The reporting system should accurately report the evaluation to the parents and students.

_____Reporting should reflect what a child has learned.

_____Reporting system should be concise and efficient.

_____Affective behavior should be reported within the classroom and within the total school environment.

_____The timing of a report should allow for continued student growth.

_____Reports should be made at suitable intervals.

_____Reporting system should reflect extracurricular activities.

Evaluating

_____To do so effectively, the person evaluating should have sufficient time.

_____Evaluation needs to be a continuous process.

_____Evaluation system should serve as a motivational device.

_____Evaluation system should be objective.

_____Evaluation should measure affective behavior.

_____Evaluation system should allow for student input.

_____Evaluation should indicate the role the teacher will play in promoting student growth.

Evaluation and Reporting Systems Analysis Sheet

1. Rate each item as you think it applies to our school.

Scale

A—true to a great extent
B—true to a considerable extent
C—true to a limited extent
N—not true

		(Circle One)
1.	The evaluation program provides students with a clear understanding of exactly what they need to do in order to improve upon or correct their individual weaknesses.	A B C N
2.	Students are involved in the evaluation of their own progress.	A B C N
3.	The evaluation program includes information on each student in the areas of achievement, personal-social adjustment, physical status, interests, attitudes, work-study skills, and creative expression.	A B C N
4.	Student progress is evaluated on a continuous basis throughout the year.	A B C N
5.	Teachers use a variety of evaluation instruments and procedures, such as systematic observation, interviews, tests, anecdotal records, sociograms, and case studies.	A B C N
6.	Information about students is obtained regularly from parents and professionals.	A B C N
7.	Teachers use the information they have about students to adapt instruction to individual differences.	A B C N
8.	Teachers utilize evaluation results to facilitate and improve the learning-teaching process.	A B C N
9.	Teachers and administrators utilize evaluation results to provide continuing feedback into the questions of curriculum development and educational policy.	A B C N
10.	A comprehensive system of cumulative records including only factual and/or documented information maintained on each student.	A B C N
11.	The evaluation program is developed and evaluated cooperatively by students, parents, teachers, and administrators.	A B C N
12.	The evaluating program is consistent with the goals and philosophy of the school.	A B C N

TOTALS

Reporting Student Progress	(Circle One)
1. Reports to parents indicate the progress of each student in relation to her/his own goals, not class standing.	A B C N
2. Reports to parents provide parents with a general understanding of their child's performance and strengths within each curriculum area.	A B C N
3. Reports to parents include parent-student-teacher conferences, personal letters, telephone calls, and home visits.	A B C N
4. Reports to parents are made whenever there is a need for them rather than merely at stated intervals.	A B C N
5. The system of reporting to parents encompasses the objectives valued by the school.	A B C N
6. Reports to parents include a method or procedure for parents to communicate with the teacher.	A B C N
7. Parents, teachers, and students understand the specific objectives of each curriculum area on which students' progress is evaluated.	A B C N
8. The system of reporting to students and parents is developed and evaluated cooperatively by students, parents, teachers, and administrators.	A B C N
9. The system of reporting to parents is consistent with the goals and philosophy of the school.	A B C N
10. The system of reporting makes it obvious that there is an opportunity for the student to improve.	A B C N
TOTALS	

● Article summaries.

Ask each group to read a specific chapter in *Wad-Ja-Get?* or an article on grading. Then ask them to discuss the reading and report back the different reactions. Once the faculty begins talking about the issues, emphasize respect for different opinions and ideas. When there is a clear spectrum of opinion, about grading and its related issues, propose that the faculty devote several in-service meetings to study the facts and work on a plan to resolve differences constructively and rationally.

THE ROAD TO OZ: THE YELLOW BRICK ROAD

Over the past decade, the small number of school districts that have risked grading reform have generated much valuable information. Although Oz is still far down the yellow brick road, the grading reform movement has made progress that few anticipated. The point has now been reached where the family conference, combined with more than three dozen key elements, constitutes a reporting-evaluating system that meets the criteria for effective feedback in a personalized learning program.

Key Elements

Foster community's desire to change
Involve community in the decision-making process
Involve teachers in the decision-making process
Involve administrators in the decision-making process
Develop criteria for evaluating and reporting
Examine alternatives including pro's and con's of each option
Establish an agreed-upon school philosophy
Establish clear priorities in the teaching-learning process
Research community needs and expectations
Discuss issues openly
Obtain accord among parents, students, and faculty
Think "outside" perceptual field
Select leadership for change
Identify barriers to change including dollars
Set goals for change process
Set parameters for change process
Set nonjudgmental, trust climate for change
Make choice
Plan implementation and evaluation steps
Individualize program with appropriate materials
Work out forms
Maintain communication
Visit other schools
Develop reporting specifics
Establish sequenced skills and objectives
Make structural changes
Organize advisory systems
Develop teacher in-service
Expand parent involvement
Evaluate the process

The yellow brick road symbolizes a way that leads teachers, parents, and students toward the promise of learning options to meet personal needs. To separate the processes which make this possible is to deny that students can become creative, intelligent, and value-clear individuals who control how and what they learn. If the promise is to be realized, it is imperative to continue the quest for Oz, not just for the welfare of a few select students, but for every child in every classroom.

Appendix: Sample Forms for Reporting

Shakopee Elementary Schools
Independent School District 720

Student _____

School _____ Shakopee, Minnesota

Dear Parents:

The family, home, and school are all vital factors in the educational progress of your child. We must all work together for his/her best physical, mental, and social growth.

This progress reporting system is based on four nine-week periods. The first and third report will be a scheduled conference between parent and teacher. A written report will also be given at this time. The second and fourth report will be a written report to the parent.

Parents and teachers are encouraged to communicate at any time that might be of benefit to the student.

The number 1, 2, 3, or 4 in a box is an evaluation of your child. A careful reading of each statement is very important to gain the meaning of the number placed in each box.

1 - In the evaluation of your child a number one (1) in the box means that this skill or trait consistently occurs.

2 - A number two (2) in the box means that this skill or trait generally occurs.

3 - A number three (3) in the box means that this skill or trait sometimes occurs.

4 - A number four (4) in the box means that this skill or trait seldom occurs.

Key: 1 - Consistently -- 2 - Generally -- 3 - Sometimes -- 4 - Seldom

Evaluation Periods
1 2 3 4

Work Habits:
Follows directions correctly
Completes work on time
Is careless in doing assignments
Shows a good attitude toward learning
Works independently
Participates well in small group activities
Takes part in class discussions

Personal Development and Inter-Personal Relationship:
Displays self-confidence
Shows courtesy and consideration -
Respects authority
Is disruptive in class behavior
Has difficulty concentrating -

Health Habits:
Is careful in appearance and cleanliness
Appears to need more rest

Pupil's Progress Report
Superintendent - Dr. Robert Mayer
Elementary Principals: Virgil Mears, Donald Tarr, Richa ordstrom

Teacher _____

Grade _____ School Year _____ Grade Next Year _____

Key: 1 - Consistently -- 2 - Generally -- 3 - Sometimes -- 4 - Seldom
X - Does not apply for this period

Subject Areas
Evaluation Periods
1 2 3 4

Language:
Uses good listening skills
Expresses ideas well orally
Expresses ideas well in writing
Has difficulty using written language skills

Handwriting:
Forms letters correctly
Applies skills in daily work

Science and Health:
Understands basic concepts

Social Studies:
Understands basic concepts
Finds and uses suitable reference materials
Has difficulty in understanding maps and charts

Physical Education:
Shows cooperation
Shows poor sportsmanship
Shows growth in skills

Art:
Shows creative ability
Has difficulty in handling materials and tools

Music:
Participates in activities
Shows improvement in skills
Uses self-control in group activities

Attendance Record:
Days Present
Days Absent
Times Tardy

Separate reports for Math, Reading and Spelling

Form No. NCR-PR-23—Supreme School Supply Co., Arcadia, WI 54612

INDIAN HILL EXEMPTED VILLAGE SCHOOL DISTRICT
CINCINNATI, OHIO 45243

SHAWNEE SCHOOL

REPORT TO PARENTS

197__ 197__ School Year

I Semester II

NAME _____

TEACHER _____

TEAM _____

The school and the home share an obligation for the education of children to help them develop to their highest potential. You are cordially invited to visit the school and consult the teacher and principal in regard to the welfare and progress of your child.

This report shows our evaluation of your child's achievement and growth in knowledge, skills, attitudes and habits in different learning areas.

In the Language Arts and Mathematics learning areas, the children are generally placed in progress groups according to their ability to handle the material successfully. In the other learning areas, children are generally grouped according to their interests and needs.

By capability at this time, we mean a child's ability to handle learning experiences as determined by maturity, aptitude, interest, study habits and attention span at the time of the evaluation. By comparing capability with achievement we can determine the extent to which the child is making the most of his or her capabilities.

Categories relative to each specific learning area have been provided for appropriate check marks. No check means means that the particular category is not applicable to the child at this time. Teacher's comments, whenever appropriate, further help to describe an assessment of your child's achievement and growth in school.

Recommendation

Robert M. Baas
Principal

_____

will work with_____

during the school year 19__ - 19____

_____
Signature of Teacher

Pupil's Name

LEARNING AREA

	Needs to improve	Improving	Works well	Outstanding

SCIENCE

Concept comprehension				
Inquiry				
Research skills				

LOW   HIGH
Capability at this time

LOW   HIGH
Achievement relative to capability

SOCIAL STUDIES

Concept comprehension				
Skill in use of research materials				
Historical concepts				
Geographical concepts				
Study skills				
Research skills				
Recognition of relationships				
Factual knowledge				

LOW   HIGH
Capability at this time

LOW   HIGH
Achievement relative to capability

HABITS AND ATTITUDES

	1st Sem	2nd Sem	Total
Days Absent			
Times Tardy			

	Not yet	Some of the time	Most of the time

WORK HABITS

Listens			
Carries out directions			
Works neatly			
Works independently			
Proofreads			
Completes work			
Uses time wisely			
Cares for materials			

SOCIAL DEVELOPMENT

Self discipline			
Courtesy			
Respect for others			
Cooperation			
Self confidence			
Reliability			
Participation			
Self responsibility			
Initiative			

Pupil's Name

LEARNING AREA

	Needs to improve	Improving	Works well	Outstanding

LANGUAGE ARTS

READING
Comprehension ....
Vocabulary ....
Interest ....
Word attack skills ....
Independent reading ....
Fluency and expression (reading aloud)............

LOW _____ HIGH
Capability at this time

LOW _____ HIGH
Achievement relative to capability

ORAL EXPRESSION
Communication of ideas ....
Creativity ....
English usage ....
Participation.............................

WRITTEN EXPRESSION
Communication of ideas ....
Organization ....
English usage ....
Creativity ....
Spelling competence ....
Handwriting ....

LISTENING
Comprehension ....
Attentive listening ....
Critical listening ....

MATHEMATICS
Number facts ....
Reasoning ....
Computation ....
Concept comprehension ....
Application ....

LOW _____ HIGH
Capability at this time

LOW _____ HIGH
Achievement relative to capability

_____
Pupil's Name

LEARNING AREA

	Needs to improve	Improving	Works well	Outstanding

GENERAL MUSIC

	Needs to improve	Improving	Works well	Outstanding
Participation				
Attitude				
Response to rhythms				
Awareness of elements of music				

or

INSTRUMENTAL MUSIC

	Needs to improve	Improving	Works well	Outstanding
Participation				
General Musicianship				
Tonal awareness				
Rhythmic awareness				
Preparation of assigned work				

ART

	Needs to improve	Improving	Works well	Outstanding
Expresses ideas creatively				
Uses variety of materials constructively				
Listens to and follows directions				
Strives for self improvement				

PHYSICAL EDUCATION

	Needs to improve	Improving	Works well	Outstanding
Participation				
Motor skills				
Fitness				
Sportsmanship				
Strives for self improvement				

Distributed by: _Adirondack Mt. Humanistic Education Center_
Upper Jay, New York 12987

JUNIOR HIGH LEVEL

Comment Sheet

Name of Student _____ Date _____

    This analysis is intended to give parents a more specific report as to the areas where student achievement is lacking and where improvement should occur. A check before any item indicates that the student needs to improve in this area.

    We strongly urge parents to make an appointment with the teacher if more clarification is desired.

READING

Teacher _____

Reading Level _____

_____ Knows and uses structured analysis
_____ Knows and uses context clues
_____ Can use the dictionary effectively
_____ Can find the main idea in selections
_____ Comprehends details
_____ Can arrange related items in sequence
_____ Can relate details to the main idea
_____ Uses inferences
_____ Recognizes the difference between different types of writing: factual, opinion, imaginative
_____ Can recognize and analyze the elements of literature
_____ Adjusts reading rate to the material
_____ Can interpret graphic materials
_____ Reads orally with inflection and comprehension
_____ Does independent reading

Remarks: _____

_____

_____

ENGLISH

Teacher_____

_____Uses correct forms in speaking
_____Uses correct forms in writing
_____Masters the mechanics of writing
_____Uses appropriate idiom and diction
_____Expresses ideas effectively in written work
_____Expresses ideas effectively in oral work
_____Knows and uses various sentence patterns
_____Knows the criteria for evaluating audio-visual communication
_____Organizes information and uses it as a basis for his own writing
_____Participates in classroom discussions
_____Fulfills required assignments

Remarks: _____

_____

SPELLING

_____Teacher
_____Passes weekly spelling tests
_____Transfers correct spelling to other work
_____Recognizes relationship of various word forms
_____Can apply spelling patterns to new words
_____Fulfills required assignments

Remarks: _____

_____

HANDWRITING

Teacher_____

_____Masters letter formation
_____Develops rhythm and adequate speed in writing
_____Transfers good writing to other work
_____Fulfills assignments

Remarks: _____

_____

_____

_____

MATHEMATICS

Teacher _____

Mathematics Level _____

_____ Knows the basic facts
_____ Performs basic computational skills accurately
_____ Interprets and solves problems
_____ Demonstrates comprehension of mathematical ideas and concepts
_____ Perceives mathematical relationships
_____ Fulfills required assignments

Remarks: _____

_____

SCIENCE

Teacher _____

_____ Performs simple experiments individually and with a group
_____ Uses problem-solving techniques effectively
_____ Knows science terms
_____ Moves logically from observation to conclusion
_____ Can see relationships and make comparisons
_____ Is able to relate scientific concepts to recent developments and every-day life
_____ Masters content material
_____ Participates in classroom discussions
_____ Fulfills assignments

Remarks: _____

_____

SOCIAL STUDIES

Teacher _____

_____ Organizes information
_____ Interprets information
_____ Evaluates information
_____ Identifies similarities and differences
_____ Assesses adequacy of data
_____ Understands terms and abbreviations
_____ Interprets maps
_____ Knows how to use charts and graphs
_____ Comprehends the significance of geographical and historical facts
_____ Masters content material
_____ Participates in classroom discussions maturely
_____ Does additional reading and research
_____ Fulfills required assignments

Remarks: _____

ART

Teacher_____

_____ Uses basic art techniques
_____ Works with different media effectively
_____ Is able to express ideas in art forms
_____ Fulfills assignments

Remarks: _____

_____

MUSIC

Teacher_____

_____ Masters the music theory that is taught
_____ Participates in group singing
_____ Shows interest and enjoyment
_____ Fulfills required assignments

Remarks: _____

_____

EFFORT AND ATTITUDES TOWARD STUDY

_____

_____

_____

_____

SOCIAL HABITS AND CONDUCT

_____

_____

_____

_____

Distributed by: *Adirondack Mt. Humanistic Education Center*
                    Upper Jay, New York 12987

PROGRESS EVALUATION I

October 5, 1959

My name is_____. This is our first evaluation in Wayne Junior High School. I am in section_____. We have Miss Tunis for English and Social Studies.

We have elected officers in our class. _____ is president; _____ is vice-chairman; _____ is secretary; and_____ is treasurer. We can buy many of our school supplies here in junior high. Our school store representative is_____.

Our class has chosen topics about which we wish to do research. My topic is _____. The books which I have used in doing my research are: _____

_____

_____

We are learning to keep research data on note cards. I have written_____ note cards. Most of the class members have written note cards. My committee's note cards are due October _____.

We write two or three compositions each week. Every Monday our spelling list is made up of the words we have not been able to spell in our written work. So far, my spelling test marks have been_____, _____, and_____.

During each report card marking period, we must read two books. I am now reading_____by_____. My report of the book is due October 14.

In our classroom we have several large bulletin boards on which the students arrange displays. I have done (much, something, nothing) to help.

Each week we write our major thought for that week. The class has turned in four thought cards. I have turned in_____thought cards.

Every day we read the news summary from the *New York Times*. Our monthly scrapbooks of current events will be due the first of each month.

We also have a classroom library. We bring books and magazines for other people to share during free reading time. I have loaned___books and magazines to the class library.

Because the class is working in various fields of research, we often work in small groups. During small group sessions, I contribute (always, often, sometimes, few times, never). When we finish small group meetings, we report our problems and progress to the entire class. During large group discussions, I participate (always, often, sometimes, seldom, never).

Because much of our work is written, we practice penmanship. This term my writing has (improved, stayed the same, gotten messy).

I turn in most of my homework assignments (on time, late, not at all).

As I review my record of this first few weeks, I believe my mark for English and social studies to be A B C D E. The areas in which I must try hardest to improve are:_____

_____

_____.

I believe my conduct thus far has been (excellent, good, fair, in need of improvement, very bad.)   Miss Tunis believes my work has been (satisfactory, unsatisfactory, failing.) Teacher's comments: _____

_____

_____

Parents' comments: _____

_____

_____

Distributed by: *Adirondack Mt. Humanistic Education Center*
Upper Jay, New York 12987

PRIMARY AND INTERMEDIATE LEVEL

Comment Sheet

Name of Student _____ Date _____

    This analysis is intended to give parents a further clarification as to the progress and performance of their child. We strongly urge parents to make an appointment with the teacher if more clarification is desired.

LANGUAGE ARTS

Reading   Teacher_____

Knows and uses basic comprehension skills _____

Knows and uses basic word attack skills _____

Reads silently _____

Reads orally _____

Additional comments: _____

_____

English   Teacher_____

Expresses ideas well orally _____

Expresses ideas well in written form_____

Has good speech habits_____

Completes required assignments _____

Additional comments: _____

_____

LANGUAGE ARTS (Continued)

Spelling   Teacher_____

Masters principles of spelling   _____

Uses correct spelling consistently in all subject areas   _____

Completes weekly assignments_____

Additional comments: _____

Handwriting   Teacher_____

Masters the elements of good handwriting   _____

Consistently makes the transfer of good writing to other work_____

Completes assignments_____

_____

****

Mathematics   Teacher_____

Knows basic facts   _____

Computes accurately_____

Interprets and solves problems _____

Perceives relationships _____

Completes assignments_____

_____

****

Science   Teacher_____

Masters concepts _____

Sees relationships and makes comparisons   _____

Performs experiments individually and with group _____

Completes required assignments: _____

Additional comments: _____

_____

Social Studies   Teacher _____

Masters geographical concepts _____

Knows and uses concepts and map skills _____

Comprehends the significance of geographical and historical facts _____

Completes required assignments and projects _____

Additional comments: _____

****

Art   Teacher_____

Participates in art activities _____

Uses tools and media well _____

Demonstrates creative ability _____

Completes assignments _____

Additional comments: _____

****

Music   Teacher_____

Masters music theory _____

Shows interest, enjoyment and appreciation_____

Additional comments: _____

****

EFFORT AND STUDY HABITS

Listens to and follows directions _____

Begins work promptly and systematically_____

Has necessary equipment _____

Uses time effectively _____

Works independently _____

Accepts responsibilities _____

_____

82

SOCIAL HABITS

Respects authority _____

Cooperates with school and safety regulations _____

Practices self-control _____

Considers others _____

Is neat and orderly in personal matters_____

Recognizes the rights and property of others _____

Relates well with peers _____

****

Parent's response _____

_____

_____

_____

_____

_____

_____

****

Parents may request an interview

In response to this comment sheet, I should like an appointment with the following teachers:

_____

_____

_____

_____

Parent's Signature _____

*Distributed by: Adirondack Mt. Humanistic Education Center
Upper Jay, New York 12987*

DATE: 11/18/75

JOHN A. HANNAH MIDDLE SCHOOL
PUPIL PROGRESS REPORT

STUDENT NAME

TEAM 71   HOMEROOM 00103

REPORTING PERIOD—09/04/75 TO 11/07/75

Subject—Math
Teacher—Rob Armdt

Academic Achievement in Mathematics

Your child has met all of the objectives set for him or her for this reporting period.

Your child has satisfactorily completed:
_____Addition of whole numbers
_____Subtraction of whole numbers
_____Multiplication of whole numbers
_____Addition of fractions
_____Subtraction of fractions
_____Multiplication of fractions
_____Division of fractions

Algebra
_____Chapter One
_____Chapter Two
_____Chapter Three
_____Completed math project

Other comments in mathematics
_____Is punctual
_____Written tests reflect a high level of understanding of material
_____Has a positive attitude
_____Assumes responsibility for own learning
_____Works well independently
_____Has not completed a satisfactory number of assignments
_____Takes responsibility for completing homework assignments on
                time

Subject—Science
Teacher—Christine Johnson

Academic Achievement in Science

Your child has met all of the objectives set for him or her for this reporting period.

In the area of earth science, your student:
_____Can identify and name basic sedimentary rocks
_____Can identify and name basic igneous rocks
_____Can identify and name basic metamorphic rocks
_____Understands and recognizes the definitions of most of the earth
                science vocabulary
_____Understands the origins of each of the rock families
_____Has completed most of the required experiments dealing with the
                earth science unit

TEAM 71 (Continued)   HOMEROOM 00103

_____Can identify and name basic minerals
_____Can accurately classify rocks into their three major groups
        (i.e. sedimentary, igneous, metamorphic)

Other comments in science
_____Written tests reflect a high level of understanding of material
_____Accepts responsibillity for personal actions
_____Activities/assignments reflect good organizational skills
_____Cooperates with others
_____Takes responsibility for completing written assignments
_____Has shown that he can collect data from a scientific experiment
        and/or research materials
_____Demonstrates awareness and applies good laboratory safety habits

Subject—Communication Arts
Teacher—Helen Wagner

Academic Achievement in Communication Arts

Your child has met a satisfactory portion of the objectives set for him or her for this reporting period.

_____Is familiar with the arrangement of materials in the library
_____Has completed all book reviews
_____Uses context clues to aid comprehension
_____Demonstrates interest in building reading vocabulary
_____Generally is able to determine the main idea
_____Generally spells words correctly on spelling tests
_____On spelling final, student achieved_____percent.
_____Is enthusiastic and exhibits ability as a self-starter
_____Capable of higher quality work
_____Generally punctuates own writing appropriately
_____Has demonstrated the ability to follow directions given orally

Subject—Social Studies
Academic Achievement in Social Studies

Your child has met all of the objectives set for him or her for this reporting period.

_____Locates the states of the United States correctly
_____Spells the states of the United States correctly
_____All assignments completed
_____Has done very well on out-of-class world geography topics

On the topography term unit, your student:
_____Did a good job on the project

On the map skills unit, your student:

_____Has demonstrated very fine skills

Other comments in social studies
_____Has a positive attitude
_____Classroom behavioral skills
_____Follows class rules

TEAM 71 (Continued)   HOMEROOM 00103

Subject—Physical Education
Teacher—Linda Nelson

Achievement in Physical Education

Your child has met all of the objectives set for him or her for this reporting period.

In addition to achieving all of the objectives your child has exceeded expectations.

Football—includes individual physical skills, team skills, and
_____Passing
_____Kicking (kick-off)
_____Punt

_____Is able to demonstrate functional skill(s) when measured by instructor.
_____Is able to demonstrate use of skill(s) in a game situation.

Soccer—includes individual physical skills, team skills, and
_____Kicking
_____Passing
_____Dribbling
_____Stopping
_____Offense strategy
_____Defense strategy

_____Is able to demonstrate use of skill(s) in a game situation.

Other comments in physical education
_____Demonstrates good sportsmanship
_____Is punctual
_____Uses class time productively
_____Cooperates with others

Subject—Band
Teacher—Al Peppel

Academic Achievement in Band

Your child has met all of the objectives set for him or her for this reporting period.

_____Works up to capabilities most of the time
_____Actions displayed in class suggest that this student is highly motivated
_____General level of performance is excellent

Other comments in band

TEAM 71 (Continued)   **HOMEROOM 00103**

Subject—French
Teacher—Isabelle Shannon

Academic Achievement in French

Your child has met all of the objectives set for him or her for this reporting period.

In addition to achieving all of the objectives your child has exceeded expectations.

_____Has demonstrated linguistic aptitude through the basic skills emphasized for this reporting period.

_____Displays great enthusiams and a positive attitude toward learning.

_____Demonstrates linguistic ability and consistently puts forth sufficient effort.

Other comments in French

_____Written tests reflect a high level of understanding of material

_____Does well on oral/practical tests

_____All study and social skills are satisfactory

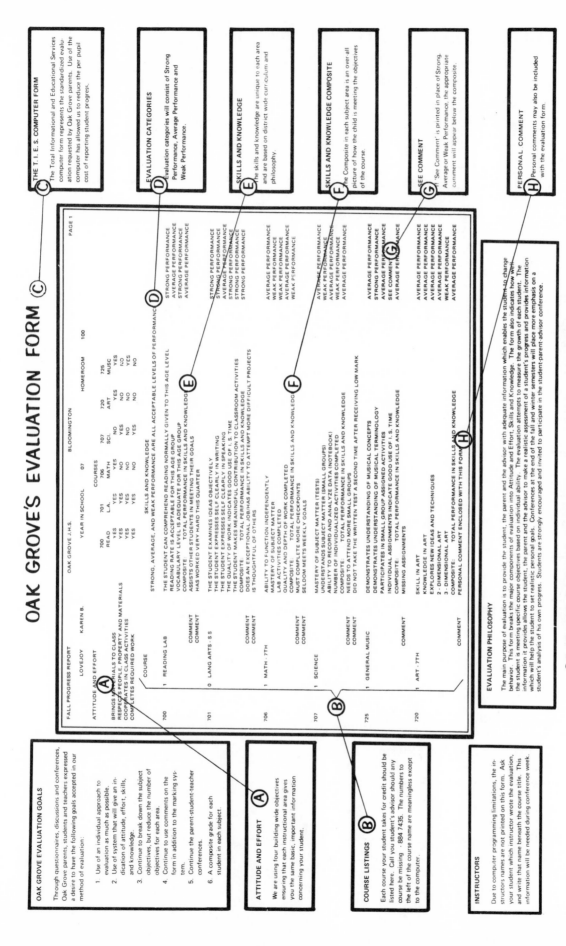

OAK GROVE'S EVALUATION FORM ©

STUDENT·PARENT·TEACHER·ADVISOR CONFERENCES COMPLEMENT THIS EVALUATION FORM

OAK GROVE EVALUATION GOALS

Through questionnaires, discussions and conferences, Oak Grove parents, students and teachers expressed a desire to have the following goals accepted in our method of evaluation:

1. Use of an individual approach to evaluation as much as possible.
2. Use of system that will give an indication of attitude, effort, skills, and knowledge.
3. Continue to break down the subject objectives, but reduce the number of objectives for each area.
4. Continue to use comments on the form in addition to the marking system.
5. Continue the parent-student-teacher conferences.
6. A composite grade for each student in each subject.

ATTITUDE AND EFFORT (A)

We are using four building wide objectives ensuring that each instructional area gives you the same basic, important information concerning your student.

COURSE LISTINGS (B)

Each course your student takes for credit should be listed here. Call you student's advisor should any course be missing - 884 7435. The numbers to the left of the course name are meaningless except to the computer.

INSTRUCTORS

Due to computer programming limitations, the instructors names are not printed on this form. Ask your student which instructor wrote the evaluation, and write that name beneath the course title. This information will be needed during conference week.

EVALUATION PHILOSOPHY

The main purpose of evaluation is to provide the student, the parent and the advisor with adequate information which enables the student to change behavior. This form breaks the major components of evaluation into Attitude and Effort, Skills and Knowledge. The form also indicates how well the student is meeting specific course objectives based on individual ability. The evaluation attempts to measure the growth of each student. The information it provides allows the student, the parent and the advisor to make a realistic assessment of a student's progress and provides information which will help the student to set realistic personal goals. Conferences at the end of the fall and winter semesters will place more emphasis on a student's analysis of his own progress. Students are strongly encouraged and invited to participate in the student-parent-advisor conference.

THE T. I. E. S. COMPUTER FORM (C)

The Total Informational and Educational Services computer form represents the standardized evaluation requested by Oak Grove parents. Use of the computer has allowed us to reduce the per pupil cost of reporting student progress.

EVALUATION CATEGORIES (D)

Evaluation categories will consist of Strong Performance, Average Performance and Weak Performance.

SKILLS AND KNOWLEDGE (E)

The skills and knowledge are unique to each area and are based on district wide curriculum and philosophy.

SKILLS AND KNOWLEDGE COMPOSITE (F)

The Composite in each subject area is an over all picture of how the child is meeting the objectives of the course.

SEE COMMENT (G)

If 'See Comment' is printed in place of Strong, Average or Weak Performance, the appropriate comment will appear below the composite.

PERSONAL COMMENT (H)

Personal comments may also be included with the evaluation form.

FALL PROGRESS REPORT   LOVEJOY   KAREN B.   OAK GROVE J.H.S.   BLOOMINGTON   PAGE 1

YEAR IN SCHOOL 07   HOMEROOM 100

COURSES

	700 READ	701 L.A.	706 MATH	707 SCI.	720 ART	725 MUSC
ATTITUDE AND EFFORT (A)						
BRINGS MATERIALS TO CLASS	YES	YES	YES	NO	YES	YES
RESPECTS PEOPLE, PROPERTY AND MATERIALS	YES	YES	YES	YES	YES	NO
COOPERATES IN CLASS ACTIVITIES	YES	YES	NO	NO	NO	YES
COMPLETES REQUIRED WORK	YES	YES	NO	NO	NO	NO

COURSE   STRONG, AVERAGE, AND WEAK PERFORMANCE ARE ALL ACCEPTABLE LEVELS OF PERFORMANCE

700 1 READING LAB
- THE STUDENT CAN COMPREHEND READING NORMALLY GIVEN TO THIS AGE LEVEL — STRONG PERFORMANCE
- READING RATE IS ACCEPTABLE FOR THIS AGE GROUP — AVERAGE PERFORMANCE
- VOCABULARY LEVEL IS ADEQUATE FOR THIS AGE GROUP — STRONG PERFORMANCE
- COMPOSITE: TOTAL PERFORMANCE IN SKILLS AND KNOWLEDGE — AVERAGE PERFORMANCE
- COMMENT: ASSISTS OTHER STUDENTS IN MEETING THEIR GOALS
- COMMENT: HAS WORKED VERY HARD THIS QUARTER

701 0 LANG ARTS - SS
- THE STUDENT EXAMINES IDEAS OBJECTIVELY — STRONG PERFORMANCE
- THE STUDENT EXPRESSES SELF CLEARLY IN WRITING — STRONG PERFORMANCE
- THE STUDENT EXPRESSES SELF CLEARLY IN SPEAKING — AVERAGE PERFORMANCE
- THE QUALITY OF WORK INDICATES GOOD USE OF L.S. TIME — STRONG PERFORMANCE
- THE STUDENT MAKES MEANINGFUL CONTRIBUTION TO CLASSROOM ACTIVITIES — STRONG PERFORMANCE
- COMPOSITE: TOTAL PERFORMANCE IN SKILLS AND KNOWLEDGE — STRONG PERFORMANCE
- COMMENT: DOES AN EXCEPTIONAL JOB/HAS ABILITY TO ATTEMPT MORE DIFFICULT PROJECTS
- COMMENT: IS THOUGHTFUL OF OTHERS

706 1 MATH - 7TH
- ABILITY TO FUNCTION INDEPENDENTLY — AVERAGE PERFORMANCE
- MASTERY OF SUBJECT MATTER — WEAK PERFORMANCE
- LAB ACTIVITIES COMPLETED — WEAK PERFORMANCE
- QUALITY AND DEPTH OF WORK COMPLETED — AVERAGE PERFORMANCE
- COMPOSITE: TOTAL PERFORMANCE IN SKILLS AND KNOWLEDGE — WEAK PERFORMANCE
- COMMENT: MUST COMPLETE MORE CHECKPOINTS
- COMMENT: SELDOM MEETS WEEKLY GOALS

707 1 SCIENCE
- MASTERY OF SUBJECT MATTER (TESTS) — AVERAGE PERFORMANCE
- UNDERSTANDS SUBJECT MATTER (SMALL GROUPS) — WEAK PERFORMANCE
- ABILITY TO RECORD AND ANALYZE DATA (NOTEBOOK) — WEAK PERFORMANCE
- NUMBER OF INDIVIDUALIZED ACTIVITIES COMPLETED — AVERAGE PERFORMANCE
- COMPOSITE: TOTAL PERFORMANCE IN SKILLS AND KNOWLEDGE — SEE COMMENT (G)
- COMMENT: NEEDS TO ATTEND MORE SMALL GROUPS
- COMMENT: DID NOT TAKE THE WRITTEN TEST A SECOND TIME AFTER RECEIVING LOW MARK

725 1 GENERAL MUSIC
- DEMONSTRATES UNDERSTANDING OF MUSICAL CONCEPTS — STRONG PERFORMANCE
- DEMONSTRATES UNDERSTANDING OF MUSICAL TERMINOLOGY — AVERAGE PERFORMANCE
- PARTICIPATES IN SMALL GROUP ASSIGNED ACTIVITIES — SEE COMMENT (G)
- INDIVIDUAL ASSIGNMENTS INDICATE GOOD USE OF L.S. TIME — AVERAGE PERFORMANCE
- COMPOSITE: TOTAL PERFORMANCE IN SKILLS AND KNOWLEDGE — AVERAGE PERFORMANCE (G)
- COMMENT: MISSING ASSIGNMENTS

720 1 ART - 7TH
- SKILL IN ART — AVERAGE PERFORMANCE
- KNOWLEDGE IN ART — AVERAGE PERFORMANCE
- EXPLORES NEW IDEAS AND TECHNIQUES — AVERAGE PERFORMANCE
- 2 - DIMENSIONAL ART — AVERAGE PERFORMANCE
- 3 - DIMENSIONAL ART — WEAK PERFORMANCE
- COMPOSITE: TOTAL PERFORMANCE IN SKILLS AND KNOWLEDGE — AVERAGE PERFORMANCE
- COMMENT: PERSONAL COMMENT ENCLOSED WITH THIS FORM (H)

SCHOOL DISTRICT #69

Junction City, Oregon
Central Elementary School

Student's Name _____ _____   Home Room Teacher _____

Grade _____   Year _____

	1	2	3	4
Days Present				
Days Absent				
Times Tardy				

Assigned to Grade _____   September 19 ____

Teacher _____

Approved _____
              Principal

KEY TO MARKING: ✓ A check indicates the skill has been taught, but not yet mastered by your child. In case of personal responsibilities, it indicates improvement is needed.

+ A plus indicates the skill has been taught and has been mastered by your child. In the case of personal responsibilities, it indicates satisfactory performance.

* An asterisk indicates a comment on the back of the page.

PERSONAL ATTITUDES AND RESPONSIBILITIES

	I	II	III	IV
Participates in Physical Education Activities . . .	☐	☐	☐	☐
Shows positive attitude in P.E.	☐	☐	☐	☐
Provides clean P.E. clothes weekly.	☐	☐	☐	☐
Takes care of personal belongings	☐	☐	☐	☐
Takes proper care of equipment and facilities . . .	☐	☐	☐	☐
Makes specific effort to help others.	☐	☐	☐	☐
Is considerate of others' feelings.	☐	☐	☐	☐
Demands reasonable share of attention	☐	☐	☐	☐
Reacts to constructive criticism well	☐	☐	☐	☐
Cooperates in small group.	☐	☐	☐	☐
Cooperates in large group	☐	☐	☐	☐
Obeys school rules.	☐	☐	☐	☐
Listens well.	☐	☐	☐	☐

Participates constructively in discussions. . . . . □ □ □ □

Is ready with attention at start of classes . . . . □ □ □ □
    (Skills, P.E., Kaleidoscope, Application)

Is ready with materials at start of classes . . . . □ □ □ □
    (Skills, P.E., Kaleidoscope, Application)

Gets assignments done on time . . . . □ □ □ □

Works well independently . . . . □ □ □ □

COMMUNICATIONS SKILLS

PUNCTUATION	I	II	III	IV
Capital Letters				
Names				
I				
Beginning of sentences.				
Calendar names.				
Greeting and closing of letter.				
Proper names				
(cities, streets, companies, schools)				
Titles of people				
Titles of stories, books, poems				
First word of direct quotation.				
First word of outline				
Periods				
End of sentence				
Initials.				
Abbreviations				
Question Marks				
Exclamation Marks				
Commas				
Day, Month, Year				
Yes, No				
City, State				
Series.				
Greeting and closing of letter.				
Direct address				
Quotations.				
Apostrophes				
Contractions.				
Possessives				
Quotation Marks				
Colons				
Business letter				
List.				

GRAMMAR
Recognizes nouns. . . . .
Recognizes pronouns . . . .
Recognizes adjectives . . . .
Recognizes verbs . . . .
Recognizes adverbs. . . . .
Can form and use correctly plural nouns . . . . . .
Can form and use correctly verb tenses. . . . . . .
Can form and use correctly comparative adjectives
Can form commonly used abbreviations. . . . . . .
Can form contractions . . . .

VOCABULARY
Homonyms. . . . .
Synonyms. . . . .

SPELLING--Level _____
Completes weekly workbook assignments accurately.
Masters weekly word list (80% mastery). . . . . . .

HANDWRITING
Correct small letter formation. . . . .
Correct capital letter formation. . . . .
Neatness and legibility in daily work . . . .

FORMS OF WRITTEN COMMUNICATION
Sentences
  Recognizes complete sentences . . . .
  Recognizes four basic sentence types. . . . . . .
  Writes four basic sentence types. . . . .
Paragraphs
  Topic sentence. . . . .
  Unity . . . .
  Sequence. . . . .
  Uses complete sentences. . . . .
  Sentence variety. . . . .
  Indentation . . . .
  Margins . . . .
Letter Writing
  Friendly letter . . . .
  Business letter . . . .

Descriptive writing. . . . .
Short story writing. . . . .
Character sketches . . . .
Poetry . . . .
Instructions/directions. . . . .
Invitations. . . . .

FORMS OF SPOKEN COMMUNICATION
Speech habits. . . . .
Introductions. . . . .
Telephone usage. . . . .
Instructions/directions. . . . .

RESEARCH AND STUDY SKILLS

	I	II	III	IV

ALPHABETIZING
first letter. . . . .
second letter . . . .
third letter. . . . .
mixed letters . . . .
book titles . . . .

INDEX
in books. . . . .
for encyclopedias . . . .

DICTIONARIES
guide words . . . .
multiple meanings . . . .
pronunciation key . . . .

OUTLINING
main topic. . . . .
subtopic. . . . .

LINE GRAPHS
making one. . . . .
using one to get information. . . . .

BAR GRAPHS
making one. . . . .
using one to get information. . . . .

CIRCLE GRAPHS
making one. . . . .
using one to get information. . . . .

TIME LINES
events in minutes . . . .
events in hours . . . .
events in years . . . .

DIAGRAMS
making one. . . . .
interpreting. . . . .

MAPS
political boundaries. . . . .
atlas . . . .
grids . . . .
latitude & longitude. . . . .
basic land forms. . . . .
basic water forms . . . .
directions. . . . .
distance scales . . . .

Parents Signature:

1st 9 weeks _____   3rd 9 weeks _____

2nd 9 weeks _____

PLEASE SIGN AND RETURN TO SCHOOL

COMMENDATION REPORT

BRAHAM MIDDLE SCHOOL

Date_____

Dear _____:

We at the Middle School feel that when a child is doing exceptionally well in a particular subject, he deserves some commendation beside a grade. We also feel that the parents appreciate being notified of this too.

Your child_____, who is in grade _____ has been doing particularly fine work in _____, and deserves appropriate recognition.

Commendation is particularly in order because:

_____Daily assignments are done neatly, correctly, and on time.

_____Active participation in class activities and discussions.

_____Independent, effective work.

_____Pleasant and cooperative attitude.

_____Extra work done voluntarily.

_____Displays a fine attitude toward school, classmates and teachers.

Additional Comments:

Sincerely,

_____
(Teacher)

_____
(Principal)

_____
(Advisor)

_____
(Student)

PLEASE USE PEN ONLY

SCHOOL RECORD FORM

Shanti School
480 Asylum Street
Hartford, Connecticut
06103

NAME _____ SEX _____
                                                        Male or Female
ADDRESS _____ PHONE _____ BIRTHDATE _____

PARENTS _____
            Father   Mother
DATE OF ENTRY _____ FROM _____
                                            School
DATE OF LEAVING _____ REASON _____

RE-ENROLLED _____ FROM _____ LEFT _____
                Date   Date

COURSE NAME	16 Points	COURSE NAME	16 Points

COURSE NAME	16 Points	COURSE NAME	16 Points

COURSE NAME	16 Points	COURSE NAME	16 Points

COURSE NAME	16 Points	COURSE NAME	16 Points

COURSE NAME	16 Points	COURSE NAME	16 Points

COURSE NAME	16 Points	COURSE NAME	16 Points

COURSE NAME	16 Points	COURSE NAME	16 Points

COURSE NAME	16 Points	COURSE NAME	16 Points

COURSE NAME	16 Points	COURSE NAME	16 Points

Graduation:

    1) 18 Credits (288 Points)
    2) Jury - 2 Cycles before graduation date
    3) G.E.D. Exam

94

OFFICIAL TRANSCRIPT

Shanti School
480 Asylum Street
Hartford, CT 06103
(203) 522-6191

STUDENT _____

COURSE NAME	INSTRUCTOR	YEAR/CYCLE	POINTS AWARDED

NUMBER OF CARNEGIE UNITS:

Eng. _____   Foreign Lang. _____
Math _____   Social Science _____
Science _____   Art _____

TOTAL: _____

TEST SCORES:

HOME GROUP LEADER	DATES

Official Signature   Position

STUDENT SELF-EVALUATION REPORT   Name _____

STUDY HABITS AND ATTITUDES	YES	NO	SOMETIMES
I exert my best effort when I work			
I work without bothering others			
I listen well			
I follow directions			
I try to finish what I start			
I take care of the things I use			
KNOWLEDGE SKILLS AND APPRECIATIONS	YES	NO	SOMETIMES
I like to share experiences			
I enjoy reading			
I read well			
I like to write reports			
I like to write stories			
I write all my work carefully			
I spell my words carefully			
I enjoy art			
I enjoy music			
I like physical education			
I am a good sport			
I enjoy math			

I have improved these math skills _____

_____

In math I am learning about _____

_____

I would like to learn more about _____

_____

FOOTNOTES AND REFERENCES

[1]Starch, Daniel, and Elliott, Edward C. "Reliability of Grading of High School Work in English." *School Review:* Volume 21; 1913.

Edward Elliott and Daniel Starch tested the reliability of grades by giving 100 teachers the same English theme to grade. The grading scale showed a 39-point spread! When the same approach was applied to science and math grades, the reliability fell even lower. Their conclusions testified to the unreliability of grading which was based on the different standards applied by individual teachers. Since that time, as often as researchers have evaluated grades, their results have supported Elliott and Starch: traditional grades are totally unreliable as measures of student progress.

[2]Glasser, William. *Schools Without Failure.* New York: Harper and Row, 1969.

[3]Rosenthal, Robert, and Jacobson, Lenore. *Pygmalion in the Classroom: Teacher Expectation and Pupils' Intellectual Development.* New York: Holt, Rinehart and Winston, 1968.

[4]Simon, Sidney; Kirschenbaum, Howard; and Napier, Rodney. *Wad-Ja-Get? The Grading Game in American Education.* New York: Hart Publishing Co., Inc., 1971.

[5]Kirschenbaum, Howard, and Bellanca, James. *The College Guide for Experimenting High Schools.* Upper Jay, N.Y.: National Humanistic Education Center, 1973.